"JUST KEEP ON KNOCKING, THE STUFF'S IN THERE"

AN ADVENTURE OF DISCOVERING WHERE MIRACLES COME FROM

ALAN SLATER

Anna,

Enjoy the journey!

Heb 10:23.

Alan & Pauline

CONTENTS

FOREWORD

"Just Keep On Knocking" is a heartwarming, faith challenging story of how God uses ordinary people to do extraordinary things.

Alan and Pauline Slater have spent most of their lives following God's leading to various ministry situations around the world. Who could have imagined the life of travel, adventure and challenge that awaited them when they set off as a young couple from their native England? This is the story of that adventure of faith, with all of its joys, disappointments, and victories.

The highlight of their journey was the fulfillment of a long-held dream of building a Christian Trade School in a developing country that would provide a place of hope and a future for young people. This dream eventually led them to Guatemala where the Lord enabled them to see it become a miraculous reality. Although their faith and vision was tested by time, circumstances and opposition, they saw it through. I so admire their faith, tenacity and perseverance in that incredible story. They have proven the truth: where God leads, He provides.

You will enjoy this very personal and transparent story and I believe it will, both inspire and encourage your faith.

Rev. Paul Cassidy.

PREFACE

'Just Keep On Knocking' was written for all readers, but especially for younger people who are looking for real evidence that miracles still happen and for those who are willing to risk all for a worthy cause. These are vignettes and stories from the lives of two very ordinary people whose journey took them into some experiences that forced them to function in a different way than most young couples. They discovered how faith works and consequently found the Source of endless supply.

In our modern, secular world, true spirituality is generally laughed off as old wives tales and legend. But here you can see that God is just as active in people's lives today as He has ever been. God is at work in His world and He is using those who are willing to be available. He has an endless supply of assignments waiting for those who are prepared to go through His 'boot camp' of training and testing in faith, which is heaven's currency, communication system and channel of supply.

Alan and Pauline started using faith early on in their lives. They set out on their adventures with blind faith, trusting that God would supply all their needs according to His riches in His storehouse. They proved this to be true by testing it over and over again. See for yourself that the life of faith is anything but boring.

Anyone who is tired of the 'status quo' kind of life should read this book, but only if you are willing to change.

ACKNOWLEDGEMENTS

There are far too many people who have influenced my life to list here. But the ones I do mention are the kind of person you would comment about by saying: "When I grow up I want to be like him".

They are; Ernest Shearman and David Newington, both of England and no longer with us. Also William Cornelius and Gary Taitinger, both of Canada. Gary is still with us and is actually younger than me in every way except for his wisdom.

These men have left deep imprints on my life for which I will be eternally grateful.

DEDICATION

To Pauline my wife and best friend.
The one who has always encouraged me to do more and has been right there with me each step of the journey.

A gift from God without which this story would be so very different.

TIME LINE OF THE JOURNEY

1946   Born and raised in Hyde, Cheshire England.

1965   Married to Pauline Hancock in Denton, Lancashire.

1967   Alan and Pauline left England for South Africa.

1972   Sailed from South Africa for Australia, then on to Papua New Guinea.

1976   Back to England and on to Ecuador, South America.

1981   Departed Ecuador for Alberta, Canada.

1995   Moved to Guatemala, Central America on 'Assignment'.

2009   Returned to Canada.

2010   Began working at The Shepherd's Care Foundation, Edmonton.

2015   Retired and moved to Kelowna, British Columbia.

CHAPTER 1

HEADING INTO
THE UNKNOWN 1995

W e went with the full intention of building a school for the underprivileged youth of Guatemala. It would be a Christian technical school for grades 10 through 12. Our target group would be boys and girls in sponsored programmes who were left stranded with nowhere to go after completing Grade 6. Other marginalized youth would also be welcome to apply.

Pauline and I knew that the Lord had given us this assignment. It would be a big challenge but what we didn't know was how life-changing this mission venture would be. Both for us and for the many people who would come to help with its construction. For those coming to run and staff the school and perhaps more importantly, for the students who would enroll and now receive an education opportunity hitherto unknown to their families and communities.

It was a brilliant summer's day in 1995 where a dozen or so of our friends and family could be seen in the carpark of our church in Mill Woods, Edmonton, Alberta, praying for us and finally sending us on our way heading due South for Guatemala City, where unbeknown to us at that time, fourteen years would be spent putting into practice the principles of faith we had been learning throughout the exciting journey we had been travelling together, since our wedding day in the October of 1965.

The day prior to our departure our dear friends Brad, Fred & Rose along with Tracy, packed all we owned into the donated school bus; and worked out the route that would take us through Alberta, Canada, the United States of America, through Mexico and finally into Guatemala heading for the capital city. Tracy our daughter would stay behind with our dog Dexter, and fly down later to Guatemala with him, once we were settled in our home there. Our son Simon was now married and in nursing school. So, after a heartfelt prayer along with tears, we set off for the southern Alberta border with Montana. This wasn't the first time we had said 'goodbye' to family and friends. Pauline and I had been part time missionaries in three other countries, responding to the Lord's call upon our lives. Only now as we look back, do we see how in each step of our journey, we were being prepared in our hearts for the challenges and frustrations that lay ahead.

We decided against fixing deadlines for this trip south, choosing instead to take our time and enjoy the journey. The officer at the Montana gate crossing was friendly and wished us well once he knew why we were driving this old bus, full of boxes and bags to Guatemala. As we pulled away, entering the United States, I remember Pauline saying, "Thank You Lord, one down, two to go!" Meaning that this particular journey would take us through three international borders, with the possibility of each one presenting its own difficulties for us to overcome. As we turned our eyes heavenward we saw a beautiful rainbow in the sky, reminding us of God's promises knowing that He would be with us every mile of the way. Our eyes glistened with tears.

We were as prepared as we could be, both from a practical point of view and spiritual. I felt, I think, like Oliver Cromwell must have, when he and his 'round head's' were confronted with having to cross an unavoidable swelling river; his command to his men was, "Have faith lads and keep your powder dry". Our passports were in order we had a letter of recognition from our mission body in Canada along with a letter of invitation from the church people in Guatemala. But, we still had to go through the process of trusting the Lord one step at a time, in order to accomplish this assignment. These would be faith steps because we had no money to build a school! Some donations had been received towards our first year in Guatemala, being sent to our missionary department in Toronto. The bus was our immediate mode of transport but was to be given to the child sponsorship office in Guatemala City on our arrival. Missionary friends in Guatemala were already in the process of finding us a place to live. So the practicalities of what we were endeavouring to do were basically in place, even though we truly had no idea what we were going to do in order to see our vision realized. We did however know how to pray. One of the things our missionary mentor David Newington had taught us, during our first years of missionary work, twenty seven years earlier in South Africa, was to bathe everything in prayer and fasting. The Church in the western world doesn't seem to see fasting as relevant today but when the way gets rough, when food becomes scarce, when the enemy of our souls is throwing his weight around, prayer and fasting proves to be a comfort to our spiritual confidence; a booster to our faith, a reminder to us in the fight, that in Christ we are more than conquerors.

So, spiritually we were ready because apart from having a strong faith in the One who promised that He would never leave us nor forsake us, it was our regular habit to fast every Wednesday. This meant having no food from Tuesday night until Thursday morning. And when things got really tough, we would simply extend our fasting accordingly, taking only fluids until there was a breakthrough.

There were times in Guatemala when even some of our missionary friends thought we were going too far suggesting that maybe it was time for us to move on and go somewhere else. Pauline and I didn't mind these well-meaning overtures from friends who were genuinely concerned for us, but we just smiled and let it go, because we knew that the Lord had given us some very strong and clear promises that this was His work and He would provide everything we need to complete it. But, more on this later....

Our drive through the States went smoothly, stopping at different places along the way, enjoying it, as a holiday. We were heading for the Texas/Laredo gate at the border with Mexico. Our intent was to visit missionary friends in Mexico City but once Mexican immigration knew our destination was Guatemala we were designated 'In Transit', meaning we were only permitted to travel through Mexico by way of the 'Transit Route'. We were then told that the transit route through Mexico starts at the Brownsville/Matamoros gate and goes down the east coast to Veracruz, crossing the isthmus via Acayucan to Juchitan. From there we would go east along the south coast to Ciudad Hidalgo, where we would eventually cross into Guatemala.

Having lived in Ecuador for several years in the late seventies, we still had a little Spanish, which we found helpful as we travelled across Texas. Travelling in Mexico as a tourist is

21

one thing; wanting to go through Mexico as a driver in 'transit' is a completely different thing. Once in Brownsville, Texas, we found that we needed to get some transit paperwork completed. This could only be done by hiring an agent, who was authorized to prepare a detailed list in Spanish of everything in the vehicle.

Three days later we joined the huge line up of vehicles that like us, was waiting to enter Mexico in order to traverse through on their way to Guatemala or El Salvador, Honduras, Costa Rica, Panama and even into South America.

Four days later we were lining up again at the Tecun Uman border crossing with Guatemala. The temperature was around 35°c, being at sea level the humidity was excessive. We waited half a day only to be told that the power had gone out and no further entries would happen until the following day! Those who could, searched around for a safe place to spend the night. A young muchacho (boy) actually came to me and informed me that his family had a place with a courtyard where we could park the bus for the night. It was a tight squeeze but it worked. Sleep evaded us that night, most likely because of the stifling heat, along with noisy mosquitoes and the sounds coming from the circle of rooms around the central toilet, which was separated only by louvered windows, with opaque glass.

Early the next morning, again we joined the line of vehicles, after spending time with the Lord, asking that His presence be with us as we maneuvered through the day. It was mid-after-noon before we were able to make our way to the Guatemalan inspection yard. This consisted of six lanes of all kinds of vehicles, sweltering with heat and human emotion as men made their appeals and arguments as to why they should be exempt from the myriad arbitrary taxes and duties being levied at them. One of the rules Pauline and I had decided to abide by in honour to the Lord, as this was His work we were about, was that we would pay no bribes. In our conversations with fellow travellers that day as we slowly made our way ever closer to the inspection yard, we heard the horror stories of taxes being demanded from the unfortunates, like ourselves, who were bringing large amounts of goods into the country. There was no consideration that these items were used, personal effects and not for resale.

Now it was our turn. We were asked by a young uniformed man, for our paperwork. This consisted of my driving license and registration, our visas, which had been stamped into our passports at the immigration shed an hour earlier and the completed Spanish version of the contents of the vehicle. At this point it was now three weeks since we had packed our clothing into black garbage bags, Pauline's crockery and kitchenware into cardboard boxes along with my books and tools. We mentioned to him that there was a large number of boxes in the bus as I opened the back door. The officer gasped and burst out laughing when we told him the number was sixty five in total. It was only at this moment we realized that each item had to be checked and given a value in order for the import duty to be charged. His next words were rapid and high pitched. I looked at him with an "I haven't a clue what you just said" look on my face. He turned and walked away. Pauline and I were left standing there, nervously smiling at each other, wondering what would happen next.

This pause in the procedure did give me an opportunity to watch what was transpiring with other drivers ahead of me. Most it seemed, were simply being given a stamped and signed document which they then took to a National Bank nearby. After showing the import duty had been paid, they were directed to another line of vehicles which, again for a fee, was profusely sprayed inside and out, with some kind of bug spray. Now my stress level increased, though not because of the clouds of bug spray baptizing the cars up front, but because I caught sight of the inspector coming out of the office building followed by his superior. He was gesticulating with his arms raised, describing the boxes and bags filling our school bus, all the way to the ceiling. Pauline and I were now quietly asking the Lord to undertake for us in this situation, knowing only too well, the amount of money I had in my money belt. This was needed to see us through until we could set up a bank account in Guatemala City.

There was a look of disbelief and incredulity on the face of the senior officer, on seeing the mountain of 'things' we had. After raising his shoulders, he then said something to the junior officer- then walked away. The younger officer gave me a sheet of 'Inspected' stickers, asking me what I thought we should pay. I needed to ask him a second time to confirm what he had said. I couldn't believe it. He said; "How much money can you pay?" My first response was $40.00 –"Not enough" he said. My final response was $50.00."Okay" was his reply, I gave him the money, he stamped and signed the import form after which Pauline and I set about putting the 'Inspected' stickers on each of the items that we could reach. Another fee for fumigation was $8.00, this was done and we drove away from that hive of nervous anxiety, with gratitude to the Lord and a pair of splitting headaches. The darkness was gathering in; we pulled into the first hotel we saw and collapsed on the bed in tears, thanking the Lord for His goodness to us on this momentous day.

The following morning was equally hot and humid, but our journey was now different. We showered, ate our first Guatemalan breakfast and the blinding headaches had gone. Now we set our eyes towards Guatemala City, across the southern route. Our next port of call was for lunch in Esquintla. The beauty of the country so far was very soothing to the eyes. Lush, semi-tropical countryside with plantations as far as the eye could see. Guatemala is rich in agriculture with abundant exports in sugar, bananas, coffee and corn, not to mention it's variety of fruits, spices and vegetables. Yet it ranks as one of the poorest countries per capita in the western hemisphere. This is mainly due to the historic divide between the extremes of wealth and poverty. Pauline and I were aware of the fact that Guatemala's 36 year civil war was finally grinding to a halt. By the time we reached Guatemala City, we had passed through four police and army road blocks. We saw armed guards everywhere, not only outside and inside Banks but even riding shotgun on soda pop trucks.

Guatemala is a lovely country with good and friendly people, but it also suffers from inordinate levels of corruption and violence. This is predominantly gang and drug related and feeds so easily on the deprivations of the poor. In going there to establish a Christian technical and High School, we knew we wouldn't be able to change such a deeply ingrained negative culture, but, we also went with the full intention of having a mighty good try.

There are many wonderful churches and ministries working hard for the sake of Christ and His Kingdom, all across the nation of Guatemala, yet the culture of corruption and lawlessness runs rampant just below the surface in spite of and in competition with the well documented high level of evangelicals in the country. It's a clear example of spiritual warfare being waged against a country that God has made a promise to bless.

In Genesis 12: 1-3 when God called Abram to leave the country of his birth and go to the land of Canaan where he would become the father of a great nation, God said, "I will bless you. And make your name great; and you shall be a blessing. I will bless those who bless you. And curse him who curses you; and in you all the families of the earth shall be blessed". In 1948, the United Nations were recognizing Israel as a nation, the vote was even, giving Guatemala the casting vote. "YES!" Guatemala said. And Israel became a nation once again, quite certainly in accordance with the will and timing of God. Guatemala has experienced a constant barrage of internal conflict ever since that vote was cast on behalf of Israel. Yet, God has lovingly been drawing this little country closer to Himself by His grace, even as the enemy has come flooding in against it.

Another observable reason that Guatemala has such a large section of its population falling into the category of extremely poor is its historical lack of focus on education for all. For several decades for political reasons, this was by design. Now with the signing of the 'Peace Treaty' this is no longer the case. So any effort to help improve the educational land-scape in this land of Eternal Spring as it is known, can only be seen as a real blessing from the Lord. Especially a school where young men and women will be able to first, catch up on their mathematics and language skills, then head into the three years of High School, as well as learn a profession or trade. Yet there are two important aspects of our vision that separate what we wanted to do in the establishment of this school from the rest.

First, as a Christian school we wanted to provide open opportunities for the students to experience what it means to be a follower of Christ. So with absolutely no pressure, we would make it clear up front to the applicants and their parents or guardian, that the school would include prayer, Bible reading and corporate worship into the weekly curriculum. Secondly, we would do all we could to make sponsorships available to all those who came to us from circumstances where it was impossible for them to pay the usual school fees.

However the vision of what this new kind of school would be like, was not new. The Lord dropped the idea into my mind while walking through the grounds of a Baptist mission station in South Africa. It was the spring of 1970. Pauline and I belonged to a British Assembly of God missionary organization called 'Lifeline to Africa' and the Lifeliners (as we were called) had been invited to a wedding. We were all 'part time missionaries'. Each one would work in our own profession or trade and serve wherever the Lord would use us during the weekends. I was a 'Fitter and Machinist' by trade having completed an excellent apprenticeship in England. As I was walking past the mission station workshop, I saw a man working on a small engine on the work bench. I turned to Pauline and said "Wouldn't it be great if, one day we could have a trade school where students could learn a skillful trade while at the same time, be discipled in the things of God?"

This seemed like a really good idea then and the thought never went away. In fact, as we moved forward in our missionary journey, working in several other countries, I remained on the lookout for the opportunity, when it might be the right time in the providence of God, to make this dream a reality.

Our loving heavenly Father has graciously led us and allowed us to serve Him in South Africa, Papua New Guinea and Ecuador. Each one for the duration of five years, Pauline working in secretarial positions and I as a machinist technician.

Our children Simon and Tracy travelled with us of course and did their schooling in whichever country we found ourselves. This was not always easy for them for obvious reasons, so we tried to make our moves to coincide with the start of the school year.

At the conclusion of our time spent in Ecuador, we moved to Canada and settled in Edmonton, Alberta. We didn't think our missionary years were over by any means, but we wanted to give Simon and Tracy some stability at this important time in their lives. Simon was 14 years old and Tracy was 12.

Pauline soon found a position as the manager of a busy 'Walk in clinic', working in the reception area for a number of doctors. I was enjoying my work as a machinist technician in the Physics department at the University of Alberta.

We quickly settled into Canadian life (Edmonton winters not withstanding) and soon found ourselves fully absorbed into the local church life of the vibrant Mill Woods Pentecostal Assembly in south east Edmonton. The Lord was so gracious and kind to bring us to this warm and loving assembly of His people. We were truly made to feel quite at home. This has been our experience as we travelled around the world; wherever we found ourselves the family of God opened their hearts, befriended us, showing their love and making us feel 'at home'.

We loved the people and the Pastor. There were opportunities to be of help to others in drawing closer to the Lord, we knew that we too were growing in our faith and trust, and that our lives were still being directed in His service.

Another 5 year period passed by before we as a family were swearing allegiance to the Queen as we became Canadian citizens.

And then, another major change took place which would shock our church family to the core and eventually confront the Slater family with the challenge of entering into pastoral ministry fulltime. In 1987, our senior Pastor, Wally Riehl went home to be with the Lord, at the young age of 43 following a series of severe heart attacks; we were all shocked and broken hearted. The assistant Pastor Gary Taitinger was soon unanimously voted in as the new senior pastor, as the church held strong in the love of God.

It was at the time of Pastor Wally's illness that Pauline and I had been seeking the Lord as to the possibility of once again, going to the mission field, especially with the desire to be involved with the establishment of a Christian trade school. Yet we were content to wait for this to happen until we were certain that both Simon and Tracy were trained in some profession and heading for self-sufficiency. But when Pastor Wally became hospitalized, we decided to put our plans on hold indefinitely in order to help Pastor Gary and our congregation to maintain stability, as we all passed through this time of shaking.

It was only a couple of months after Pastor Gary became our senior pastor, that we had a visit from Gary and his wife Carrie, to our 'Discovery Group' our exciting mid-week Bible study for new believers. They stayed until everyone had finished enjoying fellowship then dropped 'the bombshell' on us both. They wanted me to consider joining the church staff as an associate pastor. This was definitely not what we had in mind for the next phase of our lives. We were sure the Lord had another assignment for us, somewhere. But, here we were; needing to know if this was what God was doing in our lives or should we just turn away and do what we thought best. We promised to seek the Lord in this matter, which to us meant an intensive period of fasting and prayer. Listening for the voice of the Lord, through the reading and preaching of His Word and not least, being sensitive to the way the Holy Spirit speaks to us quite simply; into our hearts and minds. As the days went by, I felt at peace about the possibility of this new challenge of full time ministry. Pauline had a much more difficult time of this, but finally she found the assurance of God's hand being on what was happening to us the following Sunday after 'the visit' of Pastor Gary to our home.

Now, only in hindsight, can we see God's marvelous plan and purpose in the way things have unfolded in our lives. Spending the next eight years as an associate pastor under Pastor Gary's leadership caused me and in some cases, forced me to stretch and learn so many good, wholesome and practical things. Things that would become valuable assets in the future as we would find ourselves having to deal with constant challenges and difficulties in our ministry for the Lord on the Guatemalan project.

The Mill Woods church was growing and entering into a relocation phase, a hive of activity and planning. Yet, Pauline and I were sensing that familiar feeling within our hearts once again. We call it 'the unsettling feeling'! It's not a negative thing, but rather a sense that it's time to start to let go of the areas of service that have either been self-propagating or have outlived their productivity for the Kingdom of God. It's really only when we start to think that a particular ministry is ours, that the Holy Spirit will distance Himself from it. But, when we serve and operate with the understanding that what God has given us to do is still His and not ours, that ministry can prosper. And when the Lord desires to move His servants on to do another assignment, making a move is not difficult. It was at this time that missionary friends of ours came to visit our church, on furlough from Guatemala. They were heading up the Child Care Plus sponsorship programme of the P.A.O.C.-E.R.D.O. in Guatemala. There were a dozen schools in 1992 with children being sponsored from both Canada and also churches in the U.S. These Christian schools provided classes grade 1 through to 6.

After the Sunday evening service, the conversation with our friends over dessert and tea, had us listening to the need for a school in Guatemala, where the students could do their high school grades as well as learn practical skills! Pauline and I listened intently to what was being shared. My heart was beating ever so fast; I said "You guys have no idea what's going on in our hearts right now. For a while, we have been fasting and praying for a new assignment, the description of the need in Guatemala has been brewing in my heart for twenty five years!"

And so after much prayer and preparation, with a knowing assurance in our heart that this was what the Lord wanted us to do, here we were, in Guatemala, enjoying a 'Chapin' lunch in our first day in the country that would become 'home' for the next fourteen years. Esquintla to Guatemala City took another hour and a half. The excitement of driving to our destination was only slightly tempered by the realization in our hearts as to the enormity of the task that lay before us. We were kept quite busy however; spending that first night with our friends, we used the following day to unpack the bus, to find bedroom furniture and other basic pieces of furniture to set up home in Zone 12 of Guatemala City.

CHAPTER 2

TAKE HIM AT HIS WORD

Moving to another country in response to God's call on our lives, was not a new experience for Pauline and I, as mentioned previously, we departed from England in 1967, moving to Johannesburg, South Africa.

Being in our early twenties, we were quite unprepared for how tough life can be on young, idealistic greenhorns that we were. We arrived in Capetown with $60.00 to our name.

Most would see this as foolish, but we were simply trusting the Lord. Before we left England the Lord had told us that He would provide us with all that we needed to do His work and now here we were starting out and God has never failed us.

We quickly learned though, that He expects us to do our part in cooperating with Him, in working out His plan and purpose for our lives. In procuring work and a place to live as well as getting involved in a productive area of ministry.

Also, we began to realize that the 'testing of our faith' doesn't actually come to an end. God by His grace, keeps the tests coming our way. I can only imagine that He does this only for our good and the strengthening of our faith. Now, in our older years, when the tests come our way, we are able to handle them with more grace and patience.

Two years into our sojourn in the magnificent country of South Africa, found us settled and greatly fulfilled with a busy circuit of weekend services on the villages dotted around the beautiful little town of Nelspruit in the Eastern Transvaal. It was on a trip back from one of these outdoor services, that we experienced what can only be described as a miracle.

Responding to a request to come and share a gospel message to the workers of a large game farm, we left early in order to pick up our two African translators, getting to the farm for 10:00 a.m. The farm was situated 90 miles north of Nelspruit; in my excitement and desire to be there on time, I didn't fill the gas tank before leaving! Our journey there was very enjoyable, sharing stories with our translators, Benjamin and Enoch. Our 3 yr. old son Simon, was enjoying playing in the space behind the back seat of our 1961 Volkswagen Beetle and Tracy now 2 years old, was on Pauline's lap at the front. We arrived and our service was under a huge spreading tree; it was enjoyed by all, being followed by refreshments. It was time to leave and head home. It was my intent to fill up with gas at the next possible gas station we came to. But, what I hadn't taken into consideration was the remoteness of the area where we found ourselves. We passed a few places where a single pump was located, but each and every one was closed on Sunday. The conversation went quiet in the car, when I announced that the gas tank was on empty! We still had about 80 miles to go; it was now midafternoon, the sky was growing dark with storm clouds. Benjamin and Enoch also worked at our local filling station in Nelspruit, which I used. They were doubly troubled on hearing the news that the tank was empty; they were aware of how far away we were from home. The dark clouds seemed low enough to reach, and then huge drops of water started to hit the windshield. Cloud burst after cloudburst, filled the dirt road ahead of us. I had heard that Beetle cars could float; now we were about to find out! Sure enough, the wheels ran over the not so deep patches of the road, they would catch and we would make headway, but as we ran off the shallow parts, we simply floated along. Eventually the rain stopped, we continued on. The only sound in the car was quiet intercession and petition, that in spite of the fact we were out of gas, that we would all get back to Nelspruit safely. On and on we travelled, through farmlands and forests, long after any comments were made about running on fumes. As we pulled into the gas station in Nelspruit, it was evening. And we were loudly thanking the Lord for answering our prayers as I filled the tank. Suddenly there were whoops of excitement from Benjamin and Enoch as they watched how much was going into the tank. They knew full well that the amount of gas I put in was the absolute maximum that a V.W. Beetle can take. Having experienced all this, knowing we had travelled on an empty tank, greatly enhanced my faith and those in the car. But it also showed me something else, equally profound; that our Father in heaven is not afraid of being put to the test either! Having said that, I don't recommend anyone trying it without His say so.

Miracles are acts of God that He chooses to perform for His own purposes and for His glory. God usually uses people at these times, probably in order to help us strengthen our faith. Though we rarely understand what is happening in the spiritual realm at the time of their occurrence. We were invited to speak at a lovely little village out towards the Mozambique border and just north of the Swaziland border. We were greeted with a large crowd who had come together from several surrounding villages. The church building was the most unique I had seen. The walls, the floors and even the pulpit were covered with a beautiful light green material. Smooth as velvet.

The service went well but long. Each church group represented brought a choir piece and between each one we had introductions and various other announcements. This was obviously a 'district' meeting and we felt so privileged to be invited to participate. After about an hour and a half, the Pastor turned to me and said, "Now it's your turn!" The church was packed with more folk listening from outside and through the window openings.

Before starting to preach a simple gospel message, Pauline and I sang a duet, using the ukulele banjo. The people were thrilled to hear and enjoy these 'whites', sharing the love of God as fellow servants and followers of the Lord Jesus Christ. That even during the evil era of apartheid the family of God was clearly identifiable. It was only after I began sharing my message that I realized there would be two different translators, one into Zulu and then the other into Shangaan. The African folk expect at least an hour's sermon. There would be no problem filling their expectations this day. During the preparation of a sermon, any Pastor worth his salt will be asking the Lord to give him the theme, the words, the inspiration to be able to speak life into the hearts of his listeners. That God might use him as an instrument of blessing as the word of God is proclaimed. It is through this dynamic that even the most inexperienced preacher can be powerfully used of God.

This was my prayer, and shortly before I arrived at my concluding thoughts, a man jumped to his feet, shouting something in his local tongue at which a couple of the church elders quickly ushered him out. I noticed he was quite unkempt with matted hair and basically rags for clothes. The loud yelling continued outside for a while. Quite normally, the end of a service in Africa, is not the end of the Christian activity or event. Usually, as it was on this day, a 'healing line' would form and all who wanted prayer would be individually prayed for. This marvellous activity went on for quite a long time with God meeting the needs of those who put their faith in Him. I certainly don't claim to have the 'gift of healings', but any believer can come before the Lord and humbly exercise faith on behalf of another and that's what was happening here. As we were leaving, the Pastor mentioned that his wife had prepared a meal at their home for us and the four other Pastors who had travelled a good distance to be there today.

On the way to his house, I asked what the noisy man had been shouting during the service. The Pastor explained that the man was well known in the area and that he had been involved in witchcraft. That the demons in him yelled out in anger at what was being preached from God's word. The wonderful thing was that the two elders who escorted him out simply commanded the demons to come out in the Name of Jesus Christ, the Son of God, and immediately the man was set free from the bondage he had suffered for years. The man then told the elders and others around him that evil spirits had prevented him from washing, since placing a fetish into a sardine tin and hanging it around his neck several years previous. They then prayed together, rejoicing that he was now free and in his right mind.

The Pastor's wife and family greeted us as we walked up to the white-washed, cement block house. His wife was pleased to welcome us but looked in obvious pain. She actually had a large, silk screen coloured headscarf wrapped around her head and under her chin. Trying to be polite, we didn't ask why. We were seated around the table along with the other Pastors. Pauline was the only female at the table. All the other Pastor's wives were helping in the kitchen. The meal was delightful; consisting of a large communal bowl of vegetables in a tasty broth, a second bowl with pieces of chicken and a plate full of bread. The Bantu people of South Africa are extremely polite and kind, offering the bowls and bread to Pauline first. When the bowl with the chicken finally arrived in front of me, the only edible bits that were left were the dark meat. I let it pass by and helped myself to the vegetables. Following a prayer of blessing from the Pastor, we all tucked in and enjoyed the conversation.

There were lots of questions going backwards and forwards. I asked about the lovely coating of green velvet throughout the church. The Pastor hesitated with his answer. Chewing on his chicken just a little longer than I thought was necessary. Then, following a quick glance at his fellow Pastors, he said, "Cow dung". I tried really hard to act non-chalant, stuffing a piece of bread in my mouth and nodding as though I knew it was the latest thing in home improvements. He went on to explain how the dung is gathered up and mixed together in a big barrel with grass and water, then spread evenly over all surfaces. Two thoughts were being processed as he spoke, one was 'that explained the unusual odour as we entered the church', the other was that I hadn't had a chance to wash my hands since holding the sides of the pulpit for over an hour. I caught the cheeky glint in Pauline's eye across the table as she tucked into the large, juicy looking piece of white meat. The meal concluded with a cup of very weak Nescafe coffee, no milk or sugar. I couldn't resist any longer. I asked the Pastor why his wife was wearing the headscarf around her head. He said that she was suffering with severe toothache. I suggested that we pray for her before we leave. He called his wife to come and sit down. As she did, I stood up and said, "We are going to ask the Lord to heal your tooth". Her eyes opened wide and she yelled out something in her language. Now tears were flowing and she became excited. She was telling all within earshot that an angel had come to her in a dream the night before and said the same words that I used. The Lord and Pauline knows that I am not an angel, but this lady's faith was definitely increased by what she had experienced in the night. I prayed that the Lord would heal her tooth and the pain left her. And she then wanted everyone to know, squealing with ecstatic joy that the Lord had healed her. We all went home rejoicing at what the Lord had done that day. But that wasn't the end of the story.

A couple of days went by and Pauline developed a terrible itching feeling when going to the bathroom. We were both part time missionaries but we were also working full time. Pauline in the accounts department of a large established local fruit company known worldwide. I was working in an engine overhaul workshop not far from the famous 'Emmanuel Press' in downtown Nelspruit. As time went by, the terrible itchy feeling grew worse. So after work one day, later in the week we went to speak to a pharmacist that we knew. Pauline swallowed her pride and told him the ongoing discomfort she was feeling in the 'nether region'. He asked if we had eaten any food in the villages that we go to. She said, "Yes, I ate some chicken last Sunday with the Pastor and his family". The pharmacist explained the hygiene is not the same in the villages. That hand washing is not something everyone bothers about as water is kept for drinking, cooking and washing clothes. The itching eventually went away following a series of tablets for the treatment of 'worms!' We still laugh at how unfortunate it was for me to be left with only the dark meat. But one good thing that happened, Pauline lost seven pounds in the course of a few days. But what a way to lose it!

Occasionally, the Lifeline to Africa team would get together for fellowship. At these times, Rev. David Newington, the founder director of the part time missionary programme, would share an encouraging teaching session from God's Word as well as his profound thoughts on what new areas of ministry were opening up for outreach possibilities. At one such gathering in Durban, I was taking care of the children at the back of the room and Pauline was sitting at the front, having fellowship with her fellow wives, whom she hadn't seen in a while. David began to talk about an opportunity opening in Papua New Guinea. I was listening but not too intently, as I wanted to keep our two little ones occupied. But all of a sudden, I began to weep. I tried to control myself but the more I tried to hold it in, the more I began to sob. Deeply sobbing now, I knew this must be of the Holy Spirit. Several times as a teenager, during a period of intense seeking more from God, I had experienced similar bouts of emotion where I felt completely enveloped by the Holy Spirit. This, I was sure, was something that the Holy Spirit was doing in my heart. It lasted probably ten minutes then lifted from me. Arriving back at our accommodation I told Pauline what had happened and lo and behold, she said the same thing happened to her as she sat at the front of the room. So now we knew, this was serious. God was dealing with us for sure. We were very much aware that God breaks and melts and softens the heart, before remolding it into the shape He wants it to be, in order to make it more useful; and He often uses tears it seems to help refocus our thinking. So here we were, heading back to our comfortable home situation in Nelspruit knowing full well that it wouldn't be too long before we would be redirected to another place of service, but this time we had no idea where Papua New Guinea was!

Why would God redirect us to another place? I think I know, but at the time I didn't. Pauline and I were well situated with good jobs and fulfilled in the ministry we had on the compounds and villages. We saw people coming to Jesus and occasionally, the Lord healed the sick as we exercised faith in the power of His Name. Though we did not know why the Lord was moving us on, we did know that trusting our lives and future into His hands was the best thing we could do.

We did not rush our time of planning, for this major move. In corresponding with the Australian Embassy in Pretoria, we discovered that as British subjects, we could immigrate to Australia but the process for this would take two years due to the waiting list. The other would be – we go immediately if we purchased our own tickets. We also learned that Papua New Guinea was a 'protectorate' of Australia; in order for us to reside and work in P.N.G. it would be necessary to be in Australia and secure a job from there.

We decided to sell everything we owned, pay our own way and trust God again, for the rest. Our Siamese cat was found a good home; we sold what furniture we could and the remaining items were given away. It was hard saying goodbye to our V.W. Beetle and even harder saying goodbye to our African and Indian friends but we accepted that this is par for the course, when in service for the Lord. And we were conscious of the fact that we would have many new friends up ahead wherever the journey would take us.

We took the train from Nelspruit to Johannesburg, changing there onto the train that would take us to Durban, where we would embark onto the ship The Canberra sailing for Sydney, Australia. What a marvelous trip this was. But not without its moments of stress. Simon who was now 5 years old, decided to 'escape' from the child care centre, causing a ship wide panic as loud speaker announcements were going off, crew members running around in their search for little Simon along with Pauline and me. Apparently Simon had had enough of being away from his parents so, decided to go and find them himself. He had quite the adventure. That was the last time we put our darlings in the child care centre.

There was a myriad of activities offered on board to keep everyone occupied. One evening a Cabaret was organized, giving passengers the opportunity to participate. Pauline and I were used to singing together, so we took part, singing the old spiritual, 'Farther Along', accompanied with my ukulele. Much to our surprise it was well received, even with shouts of 'Encore! Encore!

Money was minimal, because almost all of it went to the purchasing of the tickets and the rest of the journey. But we were happy and rested in the fact that God was with us and He would provide.

In His love and mercy, as I said before, He has never let us down. But on arriving in Australia, He had a special time of testing arranged for us that we will never be able to forget.

Now having said that, I am aware that there are others who have faced times of testing far, far worse than anything we have gone through. Only God knows the answers to those "Why?" questions. But regardless of the severity of the test, God is still faithful and will see you through, even if it means that the test concludes when you are standing in His wonderful presence.

It's an awesome and exciting experience to sail into the Sydney harbour on 'The Canberra' at that time the second largest ship in the world. For this little family of four, the excitement soon came to an abrupt stop, as we hit a 'reality check' after disembarking from the ship. Our plan, was to go to Papua New Guinea and serve the Lord there. But when we checked how we were doing financially, we knew that our plan, was going to take a longer way around than we had anticipated. We had $60.00 to our name, again!

One of our local churches in Sydney knew we were arriving and agreed to host us in their guest apartment for a while. Each Friday morning I would take a bus to a particular news agents, located below the West side of Sydney Harbour Bridge.

This was the only place in the city to carry the Papua New Guinea newspaper called 'The Garamut' The name being the traditional mode of communication in the jungles of the South Pacific islands. It's simply a roughly six foot length of hollowed out tree trunk, closed at both ends, with an opening at the top. The messages are sent out by hitting the rim of the drum. I would go through the job vacancy list, sending out a copy of my resume to any and all machining type positions being advertised in Port Moresby, the capital city and any other major centres in the country such as, Lae and Mt. Hagen. Time was slipping by; eventually after 6 weeks, the church needed to use the accommodation, asking us to vacate. Quite unexpectedly during this time, we had been receiving anonymous gifts as well as cheques from near and far. It was like the feeding of Elijah in the wilderness. We had never mentioned our financial situation to anyone, because we were trusting the Lord and we knew we could rely on Him no matter how things appeared. Yet we always had enough.

What we decided to do next was unthinkable in normal circumstances. Based on the simple fact that Brisbane was closer to P.N.G. than Sydney we booked bus tickets for the following morning. This was done purely by faith, as we did not have any money left! Friends at the church invited us to stay in their trailer that night, parked in their driveway, giving us a lovely evening meal. As we were concluding our meal, there was a knock on the door. It was the assistant pastor from the church. He stuck his hand out and said, "Here is an anonymous gift for you". And with that he was gone. As we counted out the notes and coins we realized it was the exact amount of money needed for the 2 adult and 2 infant tickets that we had booked to travel to Brisbane. We quietly allowed our tears of gratitude to run down our cheeks as we explained to Simon and Tracy before putting them to bed, what had just happened. We had an early start the following day, to board a bus going north. It was just a bus ride; at least we knew we were heading in the right direction. And just being on the bus, we felt the assurance that God was watching over us, even though each turn of the wheels was a reminder that we were penniless and homeless. But we were never hopeless. Upon arriving in Brisbane, our plan was to go to the 'Peoples Palace' – the Salvation Army centre, asking if we could stay until such time that we had secured a job, after which we would rent a home, eventually moving to P.N.G. as the Lord opened the door. That was the plan, because at that point in time, it was all we could see. The journey was a long one, (especially for Simon and Tracy 5 and 3 yrs. of age) taking us through the night, arriving in Brisbane around 8:00 am the following day. "Well Lord" I thought, "what is in store for us now?" 'The bus finally came to a stop; lots of people greeting friends and family. We were in no great hurry, so we took our time alighting, preparing the children for the long walk ahead.

As I stepped off the bus, turning to lift Simon and Tracy down, giving Pauline my hand to help her I heard a voice from behind me saying "Alan?" Turning I saw a perfect stranger smiling at me. I said "Yes". He introduced himself as Gerald Rowlands, explaining that he had heard we were arriving and wanted to know where we intended staying. When I said the Salvation Army, he suggested that we first go to his home and have breakfast and see what other options were available for us. We knew that he was a pastor at a church in Brisbane so we agreed. He took us to his home and introduced us to his wife, who gave us a wonderful breakfast. He gently opened the subject as to where we could live at least temporarily. He told us that the Brisbane branch of Teen Challenge had been given an old church parsonage that needed to be cleaned up so they could use it as a half-way house for kids being rescued off the streets. He asked if we would be willing to be house parents there, until something opened up in P.N.G. We joyfully said that we would.

The next thing this servant of God did was to take us to a grocery store and stock us up with at least a week's food. So we helped to establish the 'Red Hill Crash Pad' and quickly had a half dozen kids move in with us, trying to help them experience what it is like to live in a happy family. We prayed with them, sang with them, laughed and cried with them too, explaining what it means to know the Lord Jesus as their Saviour. There were those who received the Lord and were baptized at Pastor Gerald's large church. We also tried to secure jobs for them in order for them to regain their self-esteem. It wasn't long before the supply of food dwindled down. This is when another series of miracles happened.

Before leaving South Africa we had notified our family and friends in England, what we were doing, asking them to remember us in their prayers, as we stepped out upon this new leg of our journey.

When as believers we are involved in some kind of front-line activity in the work of God, it is vital that we redouble our efforts with prayer and that we boldly ask others to join us also. Why? Because we are competing for the souls of men and women, boys and girls; the enemy of our souls, Satan is doing all he can to distract spiritually hungry souls from hearing and seeing the Christian message in action. Some would say why bother at all if God knows everything anyway? It is true that God knows everything, but He wants us to be directly involved in what He is doing. He gave us such a measure of faith. In other words, the ability to trust Him, He gave us His Holy Word, the Bible and whilst He hasn't included everything in it that we would like to know He has put everything in it that we need to know.

Being engaged in the work of God requires prayer. It's a function of spiritual warfare. God has promised to answer us when we call unto Him, in some instance before we call Him. His answer may be 'Yes what you have asked is in accordance with My will and purpose'. However He may say 'No, I cannot do what you are asking for, as this would not be in your best interest'. He may also indicate that you are to wait, for with God, timing is always perfect.

Therefore we can say that through prayer we can move the powers of heaven and if that is so, what is happening when we don't pray? Nothing. For example if you have a specific need in your life but do not pray about it for one of several possible reasons, how do you expect your need to be met? If you don't pray for your own children and grandchildren to be kept safe out there in this world brimming with loud, dazzling distractions, who will? So yes we must be serious and diligent about playing our part in the world around us, in prayer.

At the 'Crash Pad' we would gather all the young residents together each evening, praying and asking the Lord to provide for our needs, along with singing and praise to God, for all His goodness to each of us. At times we were down to our last dollar or two as we prayed together in our close knit, yet growing family circle. Yet we were now sharing an excited sense of anticipation, because the Lord had never allowed us to run out of money. So often we were reminded of that verse in

Psalm 37 v 25 'I have been young, and now am old; yet I have not seen the righteous forsaken. Nor his descendants begging bread. Money would appear through the home letter box the following day, either cash, be it a few dollars or a cheque from England or South Africa. Along with these were notes to the effect that the Lord had impressed upon them to send a gift, £5.00 or R21.00 arriving on the exact day that Pauline had been praying in the bedroom, showing her empty purse. We never appealed to people for money, only to the Lord, that He would meet our need. How very aware we were of God's timing in all of this. Some of the gifts had been on the way for six to eight weeks, only to arrive on the exact day we needed them.

Please remember, especially the younger readers these things were happening in 1972 long before there was any-thing like the internet or cell phones. All communications was through 'snail mail' mainly because to make a long distance phone call would cost an arm and a leg.

As you can imagine, these events were a tremendous source of rejoicing and thanksgiving for us but especially for these young ones from the streets of downtown Brisbane, who had only known what it was to be used and then abandoned. God came through for us every time! This was now week six for us in the crash pad, during which time I had continued to write, in response to job vacancies in Papua New Guinea. Pauline and I had realized that God was not in a hurry to get us to P.N.G. we were helping these young people in sorting out their lives and we weren't being a burden to anyone. Then one Monday morning everything changed. I received a telegram from the Workshop superintendent of a large Australian engineering company in Port Moresby, asking that I give him a call immediately; this amounted to a job interview on the phone. He asked how many air tickets I would need, telling me I could pick them up at the company's Brisbane office on Friday afternoon, flying to Port Moresby the following day, Saturday.

My biggest concern at the time was wondering how I could pay for the phone call, which came to $20.00? So much happened that week. Wednesday night was our final Bible study at Pastor Gerald's church. He had met 'Mr. Uke' which I played often singing with Pauline; He asked us, would you please sing us a song on your final night. This we did, after which they took up a love offering, for ourselves and another missionary who was sharing in the service. This not only paid the long distance phone call, it actually put money in our pockets towards our upcoming relocation. We were so grateful for this help. God is faithful.

It was exciting, walking down into Brisbane that afternoon with Simon and Tracy, but what happened on our return to the crash pad was absolutely marvelous and unforgettable all rolled into one.

As we walked up the steep Red Hill Street towards the Teen Challenge halfway house we noticed a white van pulling away from the front of the house, not having any idea why. As we approached the garden gate, several of the young residents came running excitedly shouting, "Close your eyes, close your eyes!" We complied and allowed them to lead us through the house into the kitchen. We heard cupboard doors being opened, then we were told to open our eyes. What a sight to behold-all the cupboards were full to the brim and so was the fridge. There were two Teen Challenge staff members there also who we had never met. They were happy to see everyone looking pleased with the situation but also confused at our excitement of having a food delivery. They were there to plan the staff change that would happen on our departure and wanted to know what day of the week the food van usually came. We all responded that, no such delivery in the six weeks since we opened the crash pad, had ever happened. The staff members looked at each other, then with incredulity said, 'Are you saying that you have been operating the half-way house for six weeks, and no one has ever brought you any food?

Our answer was of course that the Lord had provided and that we had never gone hungry. But yes, no Teen Challenge van had delivered any food. After further enquiry it was discovered that no-one had been informed about delivering food. But we all rejoiced at the wondrous provision of God, thanking Him for giving to us this extraordinary lesson in faith. That come what may God is faithful and will supply everything we need to do the work He has called us to do.

The next morning we were once again hugging our friends and saying goodbye. It was just a couple of hours and we touched down in Port Moresby. I remember checking my pockets. We had $60.00.

CHAPTER 3

DIFFERENT CULTURE, SAME FAITH

G uatemala City 1995. The settling in period here, took quite a bit longer than it had in the previous countries we had moved to. Mainly because to function here, it was necessary to be relatively fluent in Spanish, secondly this was the first time that we would be moving without our children Simon and Tracy and the fact that I would not be starting a new job, as a full time machinist technician.

We took time to get to know our surroundings, as well as setting up our home and office (which was also in our home). We then began to get serious about learning our new language of Spanish. We were able to arrange for our teachers to come to our home, teaching us for four hours a day, one on one Monday to Friday. This worked out well for all concerned; our teachers needed to be at the National University of Guatemala every afternoon to study and prepare for their evening classes. Our home was situated in a guarded community called 'Colonia Villa Sol' which was conveniently located back to back with the University grounds.

During our busyness of studying the Spanish language, we were also learning lots of other interesting things. Things about the human condition, things about our own spiritual growth and such things as how greatly God the Father loves to communicate with His children and answer their prayers.

One of the things we seem to need to learn over and over again, is that God is right there with us in the bad as well as in the good. In fact, He permits the negative stuff to come our way because we have a better chance of drawing closer to Him when life gets tough. Let's be honest, are we as likely to turn to Him and spend quality time with Him when all is going well? Do we fast and pray as passionately when the road we travel on, is smooth. No. One of the first things we did soon after our arrival was to search around for a vehicle. Shopping isn't near as much fun downtown Guatemala City when all you have is a school bus. Parallel parking is the worst! All cars are imported into Central America, making the prices quite inflated due to the taxes. Our vet was selling his old Mitsubishi Trooper for the right price for us, so we bought it, knowing it needed a complete overhaul of the engine So we quickly got this done, feeling really pleased to be mobile with a reliable vehicle.

We were enjoying a brief visit with my father from England and Tracy, who had accompanied him from Toronto. The plan was for them to stay for Christmas. He asked if there were any Christian bookstores, in order for him to take some gifts back home. We went to one and we left the trooper locked up in the car park. We were gone for about ten minutes, returning to the carpark only to find an empty space, the car had gone! This was the first of many hard experiences we were to have in becoming acquainted with the harsh, underbelly of the criminal element of this part of the world.

It wasn't all bad of course, God was there, watching the thieves as well as watching us. We gave thanks that we were all safe; then it was back to the school bus!

That Sunday, we decided to take my father and Tracy to the El Shaddai church, as we had been told of the simultaneous translation into English. We got two sets of headphones for my father and Tracy. At this point Pauline & I had eight months of fairly intensive brain washing with the Spanish language so we felt we could enjoy the service without the translation. We were sitting at the back as we had arrived a little late. Being our first visit to El Shaddai and driving in the school bus, it took a while to find it and then of course find a place to park our vehicle. The worship was exhilarating. Worship is always good for sure but when you have at least a thousand people really wanting to express their love of the Saviour, it's absolutely magnificent. And when it's surging heavenward in Spanish, well now, that's beyond words. The singing continued for about forty minutes when everything went quiet. A lady began to speak, using a microphone. Pauline and I were listening intently to her Spanish. Tracy and dad were listening to a direct translation. She must have been a short person because it was impossible to see her, due to the crowd.

She began to prophesy. This in itself would not be unusual as the El Shaddai church is a vibrant, independent Pentecostal Church. The lady began by stating the following: "There are four gringos at the back, one is tall, with khaki pants and a white shirt, grey hair and beard, wearing glasses. The Lord wants you to know that He is aware of the difficulties you have faced, but this great work you have come here to do is His work and He will provide all that you need to complete the work. He wants you to know that He is pleased with your quiet way of worship".

We had never been here before. No one knew who we were or why we had come. Yet God in His indescribable grace spoke right into our lives and circumstances, putting our hearts at rest, setting us right in accordance with His will for the journey ahead. Only He knew what difficulties we were going to face down the road.

During that week we had faced three specific difficulties, prior to Christmas. Tracy had a medical emergency. Secondly the Ministry of Education office, which at the time was situated on the third floor of the National Palace, had misplaced our land application file, complete with six months of paper work, documenting our running around from one government department to another, requesting permits and reports. Thirdly, we had the car stolen. God knew about them all and went to the trouble of letting us know. I was trembling at the realization that the God of the universe loves me enough to actually speak into my life. Assuring us that we were on the right track, in His will and assuring us that come what may, He would provide all that we would need to do the work He had called us to do. In the meantime, we were able to borrow a vehicle and give the bus back to the Child Care Plus sponsorship ministry, eventually replacing the Trooper with a Ford Aerostar that hopefully wouldn't be too high on the robber's list of favourites.

Eight months of Spanish lessons isn't enough of course, but we were biting at the bit to get going on the as of yet, mysterious process of acquiring a piece of land where a Christian technical school could be built. The reality is, the application can only begin and start to gain speed once the formal lessons and pressure of doing tests and exams and hours of homework are over. Becoming immersed into the community, where it is necessary to form sentences trying to make yourself understood and not being too worried about making mistakes. But like anything else that is worth doing well, learning never ends.

The learning curve in going to another country for an extended period of time in order to establish a centre of tertiary education, was about to begin. How thankful we were for the many who were praying for us and for those who were supporting us financially. Yet in all honesty, if the Lord had shown us up front all the difficulties and complicated distractions that we would face, I am not sure that I would have been as eager to go as I was. It was only as each challenge unfolded before us and we responded with faith and determination, that we could keep going from one obstacle to another. We saw how the Lord was working on our behalf, so obviously, we could not stop, we could not give up, it would have been an absolute insult to Him.

For instance, we were stuck for ideas on how to begin trying to find a piece of land. One major obstacle being, we did not have any money. This is not an obstacle to God of course, but it was still necessary for us to go through the process of taking those daily steps, in order for us to discover what God's detailed plan and purpose was.

As we fellowshipped with other missionaries, we went to various churches and ministries with them, in order for us to observe what the Lord was doing in the Christian community. We visited small churches with congregations of twenty to thirty people and large churches with several thousands of people. The majority of those attending would be hard working people living from hand to mouth. A few would be wealthy and many would be poor.

One such church we visited was Bethesda. A mid-sized church of about three hundred adults with about a hundred children. Pastor Sazo and his wife Tina also gave leadership to one of the grade schools that formed part of the Child Care Plus sponsorship ministry. During that Sunday morning service, the pastor invited Pauline and me to come up to the front and talk about the ministry project that we had come to Guatemala to establish. Following the service, the pastor asked me if I would like him to arrange a meeting with the mayor of Mixco, to ask for a piece of land. I said I would love to meet with the mayor at which time I would present him with a copy of my proposal for the building of the school.

Mixco is a large, densely populated city, immediately adjacent to Guatemala City. The meeting was arranged for the following week. This caused great excitement, the fact that we were actually meeting the mayor. We were told that he was a much loved personality in the city and, he was a true believer in the Lord Jesus. We met in the town square, just in front of the Town Hall. The town square has a fenced off park area where families with children can run and play among the grassy areas, colourful flower beds and various swings. Everywhere you look, regardless of the day of the week, the town square is filled on all four sides with cars, trucks and buses. Kiosks are plentiful, selling some kind of service, mainly relating to the business of the Town Hall, court house and police station. It was at this police station, where not so long ago, I reported the theft of our Mitsubishi Trooper. Parking the car is always easier I soon found out, if you give a nod of the head to one of the ever-present parking attendants that vie for your attention in these high occupancy areas of town. And unless you're feeling really generous, it's a good idea to negotiate the price for him to guard the car, before walking away. I omitted to do this once in front of one of the government offices and came back to find one of the tires flat! It's all part of the cultural learning curve.

We presented ourselves at the desk just inside the heavily guarded main entrance of the Town Hall. The three of us sat down to wait our turn. There were two guards outside the entrance, two at the top of the stairs leading to the mayor's office and two on either side of Pastor Sazo, my interpreter Harold from the mission office and myself. I remember feeling that this must be what it feels like to be arrested for some terrible crime, where all the guys with guns are under strict orders. "If he moves, shoot him!" But I survived the wait and eventually the guard at the top of the stairs pointed to us and motioned for us to proceed up the stairs. A young lady stepped forward from behind her desk, asking us to follow her. She then showed us into the mayor's modest office, where he greeted us and asked us to sit down. The young lady asked if we would like a coffee, to which our reply was, 'that would be very nice'. More cultural training for the English tea drinker!

Mayor Avram was a truly dignified, friendly but 'let's get to the point' kind of guy. He knew Pastor Sazo as they had worked together on various social issues around Mixco; so the pastor's introduction of me and what it was that Pauline and I had come here to do, certainly cut through the initial concern that this foreigner was here with some pipe-dream that didn't have a chance of bearing fruit. He took some time to review a Spanish version of my proposal and sent my head spinning by calling in his assistant, telling him to arrange a day when he could show us five pieces of land. These had been designated to be used for school buildings, we could choose the one we wanted and he would personally present our proposed project to the minister of education.

We were absolutely elated and wasted no time in thanking the Lord as well as Pastor Sazo and the mayor. Little could any of us know in 1996, how long it would be and how difficult could the process become, as we excitedly embarked deeper and deeper into the confusion, also known as 'bureaucracy' that holds a developing country like Guatemala, in its grip. But God knew and we knew, that God knew. We also knew that God is not the author of confusion. That He had a plan. That he wanted us to trust Him and simply move forward, come what may, until His perfect will be done.

We met with the mayor's assistant later that week, driving from one end of the municipality to the other. Mixco looks like a suburb of Guatemala City, but it is not. It is actually a city in its own right, with a population of approximately 700,000 people. Situated on the western side of Guatemala City, it spreads like tentacles along the tops and spilling down the sides of canyons and gorges. Most of the plots of land that we were shown were perched on the edges of suitable property for housing and business developments, but way too dangerous to our north American way of thinking for a school, even if you could excavate the land. The Mayor's assistant was probably hoping we would pick one of the more precarious places as these were mainly located in out of the way communities, but we just didn't feel at ease at the thought of placing a potentially large school of technology where it would be really difficult for the students to commute each day. I think he got the message, because then he took us to a parcel of land which was located right on the Mixco border with Guatemala City as well as being on the municipal bus routes between two of the major highways running into both cities; those of the San Juan and the Roosevelt. As soon as we saw it, we knew that this was the right place to build the, as yet unnamed, school project.

This piece of relatively flat land, about one and a quarter acres in size, also falls between two separate housing developments called 'colonias'. One is called Lomas de Rodeo and the other, Lomas de Cotio. When these areas were first developed in the mid-seventies, it was proper for the owner of the land to donate a portion to be used as a school. A school had never been built. It had been used illegally as a brick kiln, a land fill, a latrine, a park and a public thoroughfare. Squatters were also beginning to set up home and were it not for a family of lawyers in the neighbourhood who were treating the 'park' as treasure to be guarded at all cost, going through the acquisition process could have been even more difficult than it was.

Having said all that, I do believe that the lord was holding the land in a state of legal hibernation in order for it to be revived by a vision and a purpose that would not let go no matter how complicated the labyrinth up ahead would prove to be.

So, we had met with the mayor of Mixco who had accepted our proposal and agreed on our use of the land. The land would be 'on loan' to us 'usofructo'. This means that a contract would be drawn up between the Guatemalan Department of Lands and Properties and the church organization that we represent. This would be for a period of thirty years and as long as we are using it for a school, the contract would be renewable. The next step was to meet with the lawyer of the Administration department of the Ministry of Education.

At that meeting, whilst being served the traditional cup of Guatemalan coffee, no milk, lots of sugar, a young, slim brunette came walking into the office with such confidence, reminding me of the lawyers we see on the endless 'Law and Order' series on the T.V. She was tremendously helpful, in giving us direction as to the many steps we would need to take before being able to break sod and begin the construction phase.

She took me over to the Administration reception desk where the 'School Project' was registered and a file was opened. From this point on, any and all visits in regard to the project would be entered and stamped upon this file card. The process could now begin to move forward. Or so we thought!

Each day we would pray and ask the Lord's blessing and favour on any activity needing to be done. We would give praise and thanks for the blessings of our salvation through Christ and the promises we have through God's Word. Constantly we would be asking the Lord to keep us safe on the incredibly congested roads. Drivers in Central America do seem to have a different philosophy on exactly who has the right of way, than we do in Canada. For instance, I like to leave a space between my car and the one in front. This is an invitation to Guatemalan drivers to indicate with their steering wheel and proceed to drive into the space. It was months before I figured out that a hand making a backwards flapping motion through the driver's side window or even the passenger side meant, 'I'm coming into your lane, ready or not!' But the one habit that tested my Christian character more than any other was, the way they would come squeezing past me on the hard shoulder while waiting in a stream of traffic for our lane to start moving. They would drift along as far as they could and then the window would open and out comes the backwards flapping hand insisting that they were in a bigger hurry than everyone else. And so these times of prayer were important for the sake of our testimony and mental health.

The lawyer had provided us with a rough check-off list of the different documents that would be required by the various government departments. These 'letters' from department heads and directors were essential pieces of what turned out to be huge, complicated paper puzzles. All of which had to be chased down in order to complete the puzzle. Each one needed to be approved and signed from such offices as Engineering, Environment, Architecture, Education, Procaduria of Lands, and of course the Legal department of the Ministry of Education. But for the reader to get a better understanding of what this entailed you must consider that each of these departments had their own check off list of official 'studies' that were demanded also. Such as soil studies, community and population studies, power equipment studies, architectural code requirement studies, curriculum approvals, land studies and some questionable studies which came with suggestions that (wink, wink-nudge, nudge) "People from other countries would be willing to pay to get this approval". Often these would come by way of delays.

After going to one particular office two to three times per week for several months and seeing my file remain at the bottom of the pile, I asked the person why it was not moving along. She said, "It could be moved along but it wouldn't be the Christian thing to do". I asked what the problem was, she began to explain. "A signature from the original land owner would be needed, to move it along due to an oversight of the paperwork". I replied, "O.K. tell me who it is and I'll get the signature". She responded by telling me he was dead. This was actually a good thing because now I was able to ask the official lawyers to investigate the situation.

Nothing of this nature happens quickly anywhere I'm sure, but trying to do it while national elections are happening can also create long delays due to a new party coming into power and changing all the department heads, who often nullify previous decisions made, this requiring new permits and licenses to be sought.

During these early stages of the process, Pauline and I would go searching for these offices or I would go with one of the young men from the Child sponsorship office.

Later, as our team developed, Edna, who at that time worked at the Child sponsorship office, moving over to work with us full time, helped greatly in the work of tracking down these papers and arranging meetings with officials and lawyers. Also a big help at that time was Pastor Hector Aragon who had returned to Guatemala with his family, as a Canadian missionary along with his wife Ruth. Hector committed two days a week to assisting us with the work of tracking down these elusive sheets of stamped and signed papers and permits.

A marvelous 'God moment' happened one Saturday afternoon. I switched on the T.V. turning to the T.B.N. channel – the Trinity Broadcasting Network that was in English. I caught the end of the interview with the President of a really unique ministry called E.M.I. 'Engineering Ministries International'. He was saying that mission projects with a vision for furthering the Kingdom of God, whether schools, orphanages, clinics or hospitals, could make an application to E.M.I. for help with the architectural engineering side of the work. And if successful, could potentially receive professional assistance from engineers who have registered with E.M.I. These highly qualified engineers from all the areas of mechanical, electrical, civil, water treatment, landscaping, structural engineering and architecture, are followers of Christ who willingly donate their vacation time, airfare and skills in order to help missionaries cover the more difficult and expensive issues with the physical design and structural side of building. What a marvelous ministry! I could hardly believe my ears. I grabbed a pen, jotting down the name E.M.I. then the programme went to commercials. When the talk show host came back, the topic had changed. I called Paul, one of our American A.G. missionary friends and asked him if he could check on his computer to see if he could find an address for E.M.I. (These were the days when you could have 'dial up' for e-mails but no internet). Paul called back an hour later with the e-mail address. It was in Colorado.

June 14th, 1998- I immediately e-mailed a brief description of the project we were planning; several days later, I received a response along with quite a lengthy application form to be filled out and returned. We were in prayer constantly, so this was now added to the myriads of requests, being sent heavenward with thanksgiving and praise. As servants of the Lord, we don't get everything we ask for. If we are asking in accordance with His will, we can expect a favourable outcome or, all indications might show that we simply need to wait. If it seems that the answer is no, this could be indicating that we have asked amiss, not according to God's will, or that our motive or attitude is wrong.

Timing is everything when it comes to the will of God and God is never in a hurry, but always on time. When we know this, it makes it a whole lot easier to wait. So we waited.

In filling out the application form, we not only needed to give a detailed description of the project but we had to agree with their statement of belief. Not a problem there; as their statement ran pretty much the same as that of the denomination to which I belong, The World Missions Department of the Pentecostal Assemblies of Canada. There was also a commitment on our part to provide the airfare for the Team Leader as well as food, shelter and transport for the team of engineers during their time in country. This was all agreed by our leadership in Mississauga, Ontario.

We remained busy while we waited. Long before friends of ours set up a website for the school, we would send out a one page newsletter to all who showed an interest in the Guatemalan school project. Pauline has always been an avid communicator, no I didn't say I think she talks a lot, but anyway, she does have this gift of corresponding with so many people who have touched our lives around the world. So keeping in touch with people, churches and missions agencies all over the globe, became one of Pauline's jobs, which in turn became a source of blessing for the school. But more of this later.

I had made a personal commitment that come what may, whether waiting for permits or work teams or what, I would do something every day to move the project along. This could be, as already mentioned, running around the various government offices, chasing paperwork along or actually working on some aspect of what we envisioned the school would look like. For example; what would we need for a vocational high school? How many rooms, along with furniture and equipment? What laboratories and workshops might be needed? How many staff members might we need? Who would we get to teach Dental Hygiene, as this profession was not yet in existence in Guatemala? So, much time was spent in forward planning and envisioning for the future, so that when these questions would be discussed, we would be ready with some basic preparation already in place.

I went to measure the piece of land one day and discovered that no matter how good a plan might be for the benefit of the people, there will always be some who will fight against the plan just because it wasn't their idea in the first place.

I had hired a local architect to help me draw up an accurate size and shape of the land. While we were taking the measurements, people from the neighbourhood came over to enquire what we were doing and why? In my innocence I said that we are going to build a school for the marginalized and underprivileged young people of Guatemala. 'You can't' came the reply. 'This land belongs to us and we will fight you over it'. I simply explained that this land was designated for a school and with the mayor's approval we would be going through the legal procedures in order not to fight, but to build something that would be a benefit to all the community. Nevertheless, for the next four years we ran into many obstacles. The agitators in the community organized a tree planting campaign; the families donating and planting dozens of young trees all over the land. After seeing that this did not put us off, demonstrations were held on the land. Television crews were called to cover it and we were accused of trying to rob them of their 'park'. We were blessed with an exceptionally heavy rain storm that day, which dampened their ire, sending them home early.

It was over a month before we received the exciting news, the 'school project' had been accepted as a worthy project that had compliance with the E.M.I. policies and values. We were informed that we could now communicate with Mr. John Linquist, who would organize and lead the E.M.I. team on their trip to Guatemala. What a tremendous answer to prayer! This meant that the school would be built to North American standards and codes. This was doubly important as Guatemala is prone to earth quakes and tremors.

Our relationship with John Linquist quickly went from formal to friend. In his late sixties, his area of expertise was Horticulture. A family man, retired from the military, who had decided to serve the Lord in this unique way by joining the staff of E.M.I. – arranging teams of engineers who were willing to go anywhere to help promote the Kingdom of God. The dates of 11th to 20th September, 1998 were eventually set, with John arriving one day earlier in order to review the ten day action plan for the members of the team. We could not know at the time how wonderfully blessed we were with the personalities and calibre of this team. We had the best in the architecture,

structural, civil, water treatment, electrical, steel, and environ-
mental and of course, horticultural and landscaping.

I had previously put together a series of drawings and
rough renderings of what I thought we would need in a basic
vocational school, recalling my own experiences in the trade
school I attended as a teenager. But when these ladies and
gentlemen sat me down for a brain storming session, they
were ready with a battery of questions that kept us going for
several hours. They were brilliant in their directed lines of questioning; as they took me deeper into what it was I had been
thinking of, the picture of my vision for the school, morphed
into a much more beautiful yet practical design, utilizing the
limited amount of space at our disposal, by going up, giving
us three marvelously laid out floors while not skimping on the
garden areas.

Pauline had booked the E.M.I. team into the Wycliffe Centre
which was located in the south west suburbs of Guatemala City.
The first Sunday morning found us all at the Bethesda Church
which is located in a tough area of Mixco called 'El Milagro'
meaning 'The Miracle' This is the church previously mentioned
that also runs an excellent Christian grade school, covering
all grades from Kinder through to grade 9. Pastor Sazo is the
one who introduced me to the mayor. The church was full with
about four hundred people. As is usual, the service was lively,
leaving some of the more traditional team members wondering

what was coming next. Then Pastor Sazo invited some of the team members to come to the platform and share a greeting and an explanation as to why they had come to Guatemala. Several of the group responded including John, the leader, as well as a young married couple who came on the team; both engineers whose desire it was to use their skills in the work of the Lord wherever that may take them. Only the Lord knew at that time that this young couple would answer His call to actually move down to Guatemala to give engineering leadership to the building of the William Cornelius Vocational Training Centre.

Several times that week, we would be ensconced at the Wycliffe Centre or sat out there on that rough piece of land, discussing, planning, dreaming and developing the architectural design of what would be one of the absolute best schools in the whole country.

The team stayed for ten busy days. The architect, also called John, we found out later, was considered the best in his field in one of the large cities in the States. The Lord had truly blessed us with the 'crème de crème', for which we are always grateful. It would take a whole year before we would receive the completed set of structural drawings. Once in the country, we still had to hire a Guatemalan company to redo them, using only Guatemalan codes and this too would take another twelve months. This time was well used up with the constant paper chase that at times we thought would never come to an end. All of this was covered with prayer and fasting.

CHAPTER 4

HOW CAN YOU BE SO SURE?

B y now, it shouldn't be too hard for you as the reader to see how very determined Pauline and I were to see the enormous project through to its completion. We knew in our hearts that this was the will and work of God for us as a couple at that time.

It was firmly fixed in our minds and by faith firmly fixed in our spirits that we would not leave Guatemala until our vision of young men and women receiving an excellent education in a wholesome Christian environment, was a reality.

It was a vision that the Lord had given us and so we didn't take it personally when other people questioned whether or not we were being wise to keep trying. They saw that acquiring the land was an apparently endless struggle. That we had no financial capital to lay out for this ambitious undertaking. Some questioned our lack of experience in construction and in putting together all that would be needed in starting a technical school.

And so the question would arise; 'How can you be so sure that this is the work of God?' A legitimate question. Often coming from those who were looking at what God is doing out there in the 'mission field', perhaps with a desire to support some aspect of the work, or make a decision to join one of the 65 work teams that eventually came down from churches across Canada.

It was always a joy to share some of the many assurances that we had received from the Lord along the way. Exciting stories of how God the Holy Spirit gave us promptings and direction as we moved along our journey with our eyes fixed on Him. The following stories happened to us well before the actual building of the school began. It was at the time, when the permit to build was issued 20th September, 2000 that God's arm was outstretched and the miracles began to flow. But first let me tell you how we could be so sure that what we were doing was God's work. I've already mentioned how the Lord so dramatically spoke into our lives at that special service just before Christmas 1996 at the El Shaddai church and the unique meeting with the mayor of Mixco. Many other 'God moment' meetings took place with government officials and lawyers and people in general who on hearing what we were here to do, would point us in the right direction in order to be constantly adding to the whole structure and picture of what we needed in order to go the next step.

It was January 1999 that I went on a personal retreat to 'La Estancia'. A retreat centre operated by the 'Fraternidad' church, just outside of Guatemala City. I was able to choose a five day, Monday to Friday period when no other groups were using it. It was a large, mainly wooded area about 10 acres in size. Half was developed in a rustic type of way with several rows of dorms, a sports canopy complete with bleaches and a quaint 'A' frame chapel situated next to the camp type dining room.

The main reason I wanted to take this retreat was to spend time alone with God, in preparing my heart for the upcoming furlough Pauline and I were planning. A trip that would take us from one end of Canada to the other. I needed to prepare several talks, sermons or messages about what God is doing in this part of the world. The difficulty I felt at that time was in knowing I would be speaking in church services about world missions while having very little to show for the almost 5 years of bureaucratic run-around that I had spent so much time on.

And so, here I was at 'La Estancia' which by the way means, 'The Place'; fasting and praying, seeking the Lord for something special from Him that I could then share with the folks back home in Canada. Something that would help me report on this, as yet non-existent project, while charging the people with excitement about being involved in what God is doing in

His World. On arrival at the retreat centre around midday, I was greeted by the gate-man, Carlos. Carlos lived with his wife and two children in the small, two roomed cement block house, situated at the gate. Once inside, I was assured that I would have the whole place to myself where I could walk and talk to the Lord on rugged pathways, signposted with words such as 'Sendas de Oracion' which means, 'Pathways of Prayer'. I had a simple room with a bunk bed, a bathroom and electrical outlet where I could plug in the small kettle I took with me so I could have tea as often as necessary. I was also welcome to use the chapel whenever I wished or go for a stroll through the beautiful stand of trees that sloped down to a secure chain linked fence overlooking a deep gully and a river beyond. It was a perfect place for seeking God. Quiet and serene. The only noises coming from the singing of the birds, the occasional mosquito coming a little too close and the ubiquitous barking of dogs from the village across the ravine, up on the hillside.

I spent the remainder of the Monday trying to quieten my heart before the Lord. Calmness of heart is not something you can switch on. It's necessary to dial down the noise and pace of life in order to be in a right frame of mind when desiring to truly enter into the presence of God. Our busy lifestyle permits us generally to spend a little time each day in God's Word and in prayer, but if we are serious about hearing God's voice, then that is different. God has made Himself available to us but He is not a waiter, a bell hop or a gopher. We are to put ourselves at His disposal, not the other way round. God is Holy. As we enter into His presence it's always a good idea to come with a humble and repentant attitude. With worship and praise on our lips we need to seek God's forgiveness for any and all our sins. Those we are aware of and those we are not aware of. God knows us better than we know ourselves so there's no point in trying to enter into God's Holy presence with a back pocket full of secret sins, hoping God won't notice. His grace makes it possible for us to seek His forgiveness through what Jesus did for us on Calvary, but we are then responsible, once our spiritual eyes are open and we have been regenerated through the finished work of the Cross and the power of the Spirit, to do all we can to keep ourselves clean and ready for the Bridegroom's return. We would do well to seek God's grace on a daily basis knowing how prone we are to make bad choices. In doing so we come without fear because God's grace is sufficient. But we should never take God's grace for granted. We do not enter in with a proud or haughty attitude, but with a humble and contrite heart and in the precious Name of Jesus, we may enter in then, with boldness.

When I awoke the next morning I continued right along with my usual daily devotion time which consisted of the making of a large cup of tea, followed by the morning programme of daily Bible readings taken from the Old Testament as well as from the New Testament. My thinking is that even on a special retreat of prayer and Bible study, it's not necessary to be jumping through newfangled spiritual hoops in order to get God's attention. Just stay with the tried and tested meat and potato diet of reading God's Word and talking to Him, with the trust and belief that God will speak to us either into our hearts and minds or quicken the words of scripture to our spirit even as we are reading it.

At that time, I was reading from the book of Deuteronomy and the Gospel of St. Luke. I would read a portion and then spend time in prayer then read some more, after which I would go for a prayer walk.

Following my liquid lunch of Orange Pekoe tea -Tetley's, I made my way to the chapel to continue working my way through Deuteronomy. I was kneeling as I read chapter 28. When I got to verse 8, I sensed a check in my spirit, I stopped and read it again, it says:

> 'The Lord will command the blessing on you in your storehouses and in all to which you set your hand, and He will bless you in the land which the Lord your God is giving you.'

I know very well that this is a specific reference to the land of Israel, as Moses relays God's laws to the people of Israel;

yet the principle essence of the promise that I was sensing in my spirit at that moment was showing me that God owns everything and can still just as easily give land in Guatemala as He did in Israel. Then when I read down to verses twelve and thirteen, I was unable to read on for quite some time. The first part of verse 12 says:

> The Lord will open to you His good treasure, the heavens, to give the rain to your land in its season and to bless all the work of your hand....

Verse 13 says:

> And the Lord will make you the head and not the tail; you shall be above only, and not be beneath, if you heed the commandments of the Lord your God, which I command you today, and are careful to observe them.

I was strongly drawn to these two verses as they were presenting me with excitement and a special inner thrill of hope. Again I was aware of their historic and specific significance to God's chosen people, but as I read them repeatedly, I looked up to heaven, on my knees before God, who made these promises and said, "Oh God, what a guy wouldn't do for a promise like that!", I then continued through the rest of the chapter which spells out the consequences of disobedience. The remainder of the day was good and productive but nothing spectacular took place. The next morning was Wednesday, the middle of the retreat. I began the day with my devotion and a large cup of tea. Following a time of prayer and a careful reminder to the Lord that we were already halfway through our special time together, I began to get back to my scripture reading. I was enjoying the quiet time in the Word when I heard a gentle knock at the window. I remember feeling annoyed at this intrusion. After all, I had come to this place in order to be alone with God and perhaps, hear His still small voice. But instead, I was hearing the gate keeper's voice quietly calling; "Hermano Alan, hermano Alan", which means: "Brother Alan, brother Alan". I swallowed my annoyance and invited Carlos to come in. Carlos is a quiet, humble Christian man of Mayan origin. He is very friendly and loves to chat but after spending several previous personal retreats here at the centre, he knew how much I preferred to be left alone. Yet here he was, standing in front of me, with a well-worn Bible in his hand busily explaining, almost apologetically that the Lord had given him a verse of scripture for me that morning. I said, "Sure Carlos what is it?" While all the time thinking – 'the sooner he leaves, the sooner I can get back to seeking the face of God'. He began reading from his Spanish Bible:

And the Lord will make you the head, and not the
tail; you shall be above only, and not beneath,
if you heed the commandments of the Lord
your God, which I command you today, and are
careful to observe them.

As he began reading the scripture verse, I was immediately aware of what I had said to God the day before. "Oh God, what a guy wouldn't do for a promise like that". I began to sob, almost uncontrollably as I tried to explain to Carlos what had just happened. The sense of God's manifest presence is an awesome feeling, but it brings with it a distinct kind of fear. I believe it is the uncommon awareness of 'The Holy'. I sensed it many years ago when seeking the infilling of the Holy Spirit and only on very few other, deep spiritual encounters has the precious Holy Spirit touched my heart in such a moving way. The Lord doesn't do this simply to see us sobbing or trembling. Though these responses do seem to happen to us, especially if we are the more openly emotional types. I believe the Lord in His grace and mercy simply wishes as our loving heavenly Father, to bless us as His children with blessings, from His hand. But I also believe that this happens so rarely because we are unprepared to receive. Being busy for the Lord is not the same as being willing to sit at His feet and listen.

Carlos left the room satisfied that he had been obedient to his Master. I continued to sob.

Still heaving and trembling from the emotion of what had just happened, I made my way to the wooded area in order to give vent to praise and worship of Him who is so worthy. I also knew that I needed to press on with sermon preparation as we were to leave for Canada in five weeks. The text I was reading, as I sat on a bench just inside the wooded area, overlooking a gully and out across some fields, was from Luke's Gospel chapter 11 and verse 9 and 10. It's where Jesus is assuring His disciples that they are authorized and encouraged to ask, seek and knock when they come to the Father.

We had recently received the preliminary design work for the school and I was aware that it would require at least a million dollars to complete just the building alone. I remember looking up through the trees into the beautiful blue sky and saying, "Oh God, this is Your work, how do you plan on supplying all that we need to do the job?" Immediately, I heard a very distinct knocking noise. The sound was like the knocking on a door. I was out in the woods, no doors in sight! The knocking continued. I peered around, trying to locate the cause of the knocking. Then I saw it. About 30 feet away from where I was sitting. I saw a bird, knocking it's beak against the side of an old tree. It was especially strange because this bird was not a woodpecker it was a magpie! I was fascinated by this unusual sight and as I pondered what was taking place here, I heard a voice speaking as it was, into my mind that said, "Just keep on knocking, the stuffs in there!" I began trembling again with Holy fear. God had never spoken into my mind like this before. Everything was just the same all around me, but now I felt like I had entered another realm. I turned my head from the magpie and saw the usual scene across the ravine. Several cows were grazing on the hillside across from where I was sitting and as I looked at them the Lord said. "Do you see those cows? I own them and the cattle on a thousand hills are Mine. And the wealth in every mine belong to Me". To my recollection God had never answered a question so quickly. I was scared, filled with awe and joy, all at the same time. And all I could do was sob and thank Him over and over again.

So now with a hitherto unknown confidence, I worked on the sermon from Luke 11:9-10. It was as though I was hearing this straight from the Lord for the first time, telling me to go ahead and ask the Father in His Name. Seek Him and don't stop knocking till the door is opened. I have never felt right about asking people for financial help, especially when it's for the Lord's work. I had been pressured by some in leadership to go visit or send written requests to different foundations or to wealthy individuals. But not one gave to the school project. So I decided that we should ask only the Lord for help and simply make the needs of the school known. This way it was entirely up to the Holy Spirit to prompt the hearts of those who would give. The asking, seeking and knocking is not to be between people but from God's children to their heavenly Father.

So with several sermons in hand, Pauline and I, ready with good testimonies of God's great goodness to us in Guatemala, left for Canada. We knew that the Lord would be with us, but we could never have imagined all the wonderful assurances the Lord had in store for us as we traversed across our beautiful country. We experienced many words of encouragement communicated through the gifts of the Holy Spirit. Four stand out as being particularly dramatic in that they referred directly to the enormity and the fallout of blessing that the William Cornelius Vocational Training Centre would have on Guatemala and beyond. Again, you be the judge.

Only one of the four people delivering these divine communiques had any knowledge of who we were prior to our visit to their respective churches.

I begin with a detailed vision the Lord gave to a member of our home church, Mill Woods Pentecostal Assembly in Edmonton; Pauline and I only learned about this several weeks later, due to the fact that the vision was given in two parts and only after the second part was given, did it make sense. It was given to us in written form by the person who received it. He describes it in the following way. (His words).

"When you were giving your report on Guatemala, I believe God gave me a vision. It happened after you had finished and just after Pastor Gary said to pray specifically for the Slaters. I hadn't received the full interpretation until Camp time, (several weeks later). I was looking at a fertile dark field that had been planted, with nothing coming up. The field needed water. I saw a small sprinkler coming up from where your compound is located. It was spinning very slowly for what seemed like a very long time, I knew instantly that it was God causing this to spin, I wondered – why isn't this going faster? Gradually this started to turn faster and faster there was so much water coming out the ends. The water then burst out beside the sprinkler and sprayed much further. This water spout seemed like it had a couple of feet diameter. I felt looking at this that, wow God, You are doing a great work. The people watching this decided that the work was done. After being back in their home country many miles away, they looked back and could see this massive, massive water spout bursting into the sky with people rising up from it, seated in a driving position but without any vehicles, spreading to all corners of the sky. I was totally in awe at the massive power of God how He was using this place that you folks were involved with. I think most of this is self-explanatory but I realized the persons watching this were the Slaters. The sprinkler symbolizing the Guatemala work. At camp I believe God revealed to me that the mission will impact the world".

On another occasion following the missions service at the Kitchener church where Pastor Ken Bombay was pastoring; a lady came to Pauline and me and gave us this hand written note complete with an enthusiastic explanation. It reads:

'On Sunday May 30, 1999 in Immanuel Pentecostal Church in Kitchener, Ontario, God showed me J........., a picture in my mind of hydro-electricity running from East to West on your land in Guatemala. I shared with both of you that God speaks to me in book, chapter and verse and that on May 11, 1999 He gave me Exodus 33:14. I believe that God is using both of you to bring His light in Guatemala. May you always be in His presence'.

Exodus 33: 14 says:

And He said, "My presence will go with you, and I will give you rest".

I should point out that these were the days when we were still trying to raise our support in order to be able to stay in Guatemala. So these divinely prompted words of encouragement were an enormous comfort to us at a time when faith in the call and in the promises of God, were all we had to go on. But rather than feeling that we were heading for a disaster or that we were on a fool's errand, we were being strengthened in our faith and in our resolve.

Following a service in Evangel Church, Oakville, Ontario we were given another hand written prophetic word

It reads: August 31. Intercessory Group:

Prophetic word for Alan & Pauline Slater.
Jesus is standing right here before you today.
He knows you are happy and excited about His
work, yet He says if only you knew how filled
with joy that He is concerning this work. His joy is
great over doing His work. He is joyful to be able
to be with so many little ones, that He will be able
to spend time with in the fields, laughing and caring
for them. Be prepared says the Lord for surprises,
He will open to you many surprises to show His
excitement over you as dear children; you will walk
into many surprises sent by Him. Both great and
small. He will rebuke the devourer for your sake.

Again may I say that this is the reason Pauline and I felt we had to write this book of stories. What's coming in the next few chapters is proof of the validity, of what the Lord said to us through the many words of messages given to us during the first five years of working on this project. Some perhaps thought of them as wasted years but no, these were filled up with prayer, fasting, trusting, testing and a preparation time. All in readiness for the bursting forth of the blessings that came from all the surprises that started to manifest. One after another, then another and another. Still with challenges but accompanied with joy.

Shortly before returning to Guatemala, I had the opportunity of spending a couple of weeks with my father in England visiting our home church in Denton, Manchester where as a teenager I had attended and where Pauline and I had been sent out as missionaries to South Africa in 1967. Again as with the church mentioned in Guatemala, we were enjoying a vigorous praise and worship time, when a young man motioned to the Pastor that he had a word from the Lord. He was invited to step forward where he began to describe a work that God is going to do that will bring a great harvest. It was more of an exciting, prophetic testimony of God's wondrous power and glory in His work at extending His Kingdom. Then he stopped talking and gazed around the auditorium. His eyes eventually settled on mine and he yelled, "This is for you isn't it? This is what God is doing through your ministry!" I was once again awestruck and humbled at the way the Lord had chosen to reassure me of His ownership of this Guatemalan project. I simply nodded in response to the young man's affirmation and bowed my head in gratitude to the Master.

We returned to Guatemala, October of 1999. The Lord had provided us with the gift of a Crew Cab truck from a Christian family in Calgary, Alberta, who owned a trucking company. It was precisely what we needed for the building of the school, and having done this trip once before with the school bus, we were well prepared for the journey through the border crossings, all of which went much more smoothly this time.

Once back in the harness we got down to the work of putting together the necessary components required to set up a Christian oriented technical High school. As previously mentioned, we faced many obstacles from all sides. Many I believe contrived by the enemy of our souls and designed to discourage and stop us from accomplishing our goals. But how could we doubt the will and purpose of God after the way we had been affirmed so clearly from above? There were many other ways that the Lord so graciously showed us that this was His work and that He was behind the organizing of it.

The Lord provided our support. First, through the P.A.O.C. E.R.D.O. department, then through the P.A.O.C. Mission Link. All our monthly bills for the project were thankfully covered through the ongoing faithful giving of our friends at the Mill Woods Pentecostal Assembly. We were blessed by the technical help from the E.M.I. team members of engineers. Two of whom came back to live and serve the Lord in Guatemala, giving ongoing technical oversight to the William Cornelius project as well as giving the same professional assistance to the numerous other projects in Central America. Also it was at this time that Hector & Ruth Aragon, along with their daughters, came back to live in Guatemala. Hector becoming an important 'go-between' and translator for me in those early meetings. Then, after coming on a work team from our home church, another husband and wife team felt called to return to help with the construction work. They came with their two youngest children and were integral to the speed and success of the actual building and concrete work.

The last but not least member of our planning team the Lord gave to us, was Edna de Estrada. Edna began helping us with paperwork on a part-time basis, but later came over to work on the school project in a full time capacity having previously been working at the Child Care Plus office, prior to this move. Edna was passionate for the work of the Lord in whatever she was doing, and it became obvious to us that she was a person who had tremendous potential in leadership. Edna grew into the work of administration under Pauline's mentoring and guidance, to the point that when it was time for us to consider our role of leadership was coming to an end. It was not a difficult decision to pass the baton of school Administrator on to her.

I must mention the two churches that have continued to come alongside the school with ongoing help and assistance, they are; Evangel Pentecostal Church in Kelowna and

Millwoods Pentecostal Assembly in Edmonton. They have made possible the development of several laboratories and departments of the school, with the highest quality and practicability, promising some of the best education the Guatemalan students will find anywhere in the country.

The Lord sent to us many more highly skilled people than just the few I have mentioned. All played their part and gave willingly of their time, talents and treasure toward what we see today as the William Cornelius Vocational Training Centre. We join together in giving Him all the glory.

And so, I share these dramatic stories as illustrations of why we are absolutely sure that what we were about here, was and still is, the will and work of the Lord, in conjunction with the manifold missionary activity happening, not only in Guatemala but in all corners of the world as the Holy Spirit moves in people's hearts to simply be obedient to His call.

CHAPTER 5

PROTECTION BY HIS HAND.

B efore we begin to review the seeming odyssey of God's blatant flow of miraculous provision, it would be appropriate at this point in the story to share some of the events in our lives that helped make us who we are today.

We both grew up in ordinary, working class families in the North of England. Pauline gave her heart to the Lord at age 8, a year after her parents divorced. She knew that in Jesus, she had found someone in whom she could trust her life. Not only her life here, but also her eternal life. Her favourite hymn at that time was, 'What a friend we have in Jesus' she believed it and simply trusted her new friend, Jesus.

It was at the age of fourteen that the Lord spoke to her, informing her that one day she would be a missionary. Her mother had always said that this would not happen whilst she was alive and sadly to say, it never did; her mum passed away at the young age of forty three, leaving behind her only child at the young age of nineteen. Pauline had taken care of her mum in their home for 3 months, having those precious quality days with her, knowing it would not be for too long. The one consolation Pauline had was her mother had served the Lord for many years, drifted away, but 3 months before her passing, she prayed and asked the Lord to forgive her and she found that peace once again.

I was raised in a Christian home and accepted the Lord Jesus as my own personal Saviour at age 9.

Pauline loved her school years and was a leader among her peers at the church she attended. She was an upbeat happy kind of person, enthusiastic at home, work and play, doing well at all she put her hand to, but hadn't any siblings. I on the other hand disliked school immensely, didn't enjoy sports but developed a deep love and trust in the Lord. Being the third of four children in our home, I was aware early that accidents are a part of life and none of us are exempt from them. But I do need to share some of the extraordinary things that happened to me as a boy that really should have ended in disaster but didn't. Followed by several incidents that occurred at later times, during our life's journey.

I have two older brothers, John, 6 years my senior and Eric 2 years older than me. I am also blessed with my-forever delightful younger sister, Renee.

John had received a long bow for his 15th birthday, complete with half a dozen arrows in a quiver. He must have been in a particularly good mood that day, as he agreed to let me tag along with Eric and Cousin Roy, to 'Foleys Field' a local farmer's field about a mile from home. He wanted to do some target practice and I guess our mum didn't want him to fill the back gate with holes. John was a bit of a 'dare-devil' at times and not a little impulsive, especially in front of his present audience.

So with no real targets in sight and already being bored with just seeing how far he could shoot the arrow, he turned the bow and shot it straight up into the sky then shouted "Run!" Unfortunately I wasn't paying any attention at all as to what was happening, until I realized they were all screaming at me! I froze on the spot as my brothers and cousin watched the arrow coming straight down towards where I stood. But instead of staying in the vertical position, the arrow tilted to one side and just smacked me on the top of my head with the shaft of the arrow instead of penetrating my skull. I was now the unusual centre of attention as John and Eric busily worked at coming up with a story that would satisfy our mum as to who was responsible for the egg sized lump on Alan's head? They decided to pick on Frank Breely a local bully who they said had thrown a stone at my head. It was all we could do to stop her from going to Frank's home with the rolling pin. The lies about Frank notwithstanding, why did the arrow flip on to its side on the way down? It had a brass point and feathered flights. It should have descended vertically, if it had, I would have been dead at the age of 9.

We all attended Greenfield Secondary Modern school in Hyde, our hometown. This meant that we would leave school at age 15. When I reached 14 years of age, I took over my brother Eric's after school delivery job, at our local grocery store. I wasn't as strong as Eric, so I had quite a tough time riding the order bike. It had a heavy frame, a big wheel at the back and a small wheel at the front. The basket over the front wheel was big enough to take four boxes of groceries. Mainly dried goods, cans, jars, bottles and eggs. My working after school hours were Monday to Friday and every Saturday morning. This provided £1.00 per week extra boost for mum and dad who always seemed to be struggling to make ends meet.

The order bike was old and didn't have cable type brakes. They were operated by pulling the levers which would raise a metal ring on the front end of the brake lever. This would then pull up on a metal nipple on the top of a steel rod, this applying the brake pads to the insides of the wheel rims. What I didn't know in my youthful ignorance was that Mr. Harvard, the owner of the store, didn't think it was serious! When I informed him, he checked the brakes, and said they were fine they were fine. Apparently the wear on the rings and nipples weren't uniform so nine times out of ten they worked.

Hyde is a quaint little town, situated on the East foot hills of the Pennine Range, which runs up the centre of England and carries many examples of Roman roads. A portion is still being used on Werneth Low which was built to connect Glossop to Stockport. It's surrounded by farms but has had a rich history of industry in the areas of textiles, rubber products as well as manufacturing in steel. Being on the side of the Pennines the main road through the centre of Hyde has a steady uphill gradient. And even more so as you continue up Hyde Lane into Stockport Road, Gee Cross; just past the cemetery, to the left there is a street called Lilly Street. A steep hill which I had to go down each week after making a regular delivery. One day, as I began the descent, I applied the brakes, they did not work. By halfway down I was flying! Going way too fast to jump off. I was praying and asking the Lord to help me as I headed down to Stockport Road at a very fast rate. At 5:00 pm, Stockport Road is very busy. I steered the bike to take as large a curve as possible, going from left to right. This took place in 1960 when both sides of Lilly Street had brick terraced homes. It was impossible to see what traffic was coming in either direction on Stockport Road. So I just called out to Jesus and shot out into the big curve, right into and across the road, which meant I crossed the oncoming lane of traffic and continued down with the flow of traffic on the far side of the road. I could easily have been killed that day, but I wasn't.

This next story of preservation seems so farfetched, I've told it to very few people. On this occasion I was gliding down the main street of Hyde, Market Street. This is now Saturday morning. The road is narrow for a main street, wide enough for traffic to flow-one lane only in each direction. As I cycled past Edna Street, I could see a delivery van parked at the curb in front of Hollingsworth's Confectionary shop and a car waiting for the opportunity to go around the van. I applied the brakes......nothing! I was again loaded with boxes of groceries and going too fast to do anything but cry out, "Lord Jesus, help me!" frantically squeezing the brakes. I was now about twenty feet from the van as the delivery man pulled out a tray of fresh bread from the back racks. I closed my eyes, fully expecting to plough into the back of the van. When I opened them, I was stationery at the front end of the van, next to the curb. I looked back thinking- someone must have seen what just happened but no, the delivery man was walking toward the back of the van to get more trays. The waiting car now slowly moved around the van and continued on his way. I was stunned. I couldn't believe it, I kept it to myself. As I read in God's Word how for whatever reason, Philip was translated from one location to another (see Acts 8: 39-40) I simply acknowledged it was the Lord answering my prayer, in a miraculous manner, for whatever reason He wished. But it was something I couldn't forget. Scripture is very clear as to the function of God's messengers-the angels. There is no doubt in my mind that their finger prints are all over these events. I have learned to put my trust completely in the Lord for He is faithful in all His dealings with us. Even in those times of testing and loss, when we really don't have any true words of comfort either for ourselves or for others, I can still say; God is God, He loves you more than life's experiences permit us to understand. His will is best, so regardless of our circumstances, we wait for clarity on those inexplicable happenings. When we stand in His presence one day, answers will be available but then it won't matter.

Move forward in time now to 1968. Pauline and I had joined the 'Lifeline to Africa' Assemblies of God, U.K. missionary programme. Young professionals, singles and married, committed to live and work in South Africa, giving of their time, talent and treasure toward the marvelous Gospel outreach work, operating through the well documented network of ministries of Emanuel Press, Nelspruit, South Africa.

About a dozen of us were living and working in and around Johannesburg in our particular professions and trades, I as a machinist; our spare time was spent working with the local churches both in the 'white' communities and 'black'. Apartheid was alive and well during these years. But we were young and ignorant of much of the harsh history that had happened, even in the recent past. So whenever we had the opportunity, a group of us would go to several of the 'locations' as they were called at that time. Now known as 'Townships' such as, Soweto, Vosloorus, Katlehong Tembisa and Alexandra. We went through the process of obtaining special passes, but we were told that safety was not guaranteed and that we were on these locations at our own risk. These massive, let's call them African townships were divided mainly by ethnic or tribal groupings. Sotho, Zulu, Shangaan, Pedi, Ndebele and Xhosa come to mind.

The winding road would pass each ethnic group, one by one. The danger was great for the African worker coming home on a Friday evening with his wage in cash, having to go past one tribe after another. Many robberies would take place as they ran the gauntlet each week. Always, we were welcomed at the local churches on any of the townships. There was no apartheid in church, recognizing each other as brothers and sisters in Christ. And as long as we stayed in the car, on the road in and out, we always felt safe.

One particular Saturday morning, four of our team were invited to attend a special church service at one of the churches we regularly ministered in on the Tembisa Township. It was an evangelistic outreach to the community, so we carried with us, lots of Gospel literature in the car. We were travelling in Bill Golding's car that day, he was in his late sixties, our oldest Lifeline member.

It was now early afternoon as we were heading back along the road that skirted first one heavily populated area, then another. Our conversation was lively and exciting as we enjoyed recapping the presence of God we felt as we had shared fellowship with our African friends. Then, Bang! Without any warning, a vehicle pulled off the grass verge right into our path. We bounced off the front end of the medium sized laundry van and eventually stopped inches away from a huge rock about fifteen feet in on the other side of the road. We all checked ourselves for injuries and apart from a couple of bumped heads, we were all fine. The driver of the van was unhurt.

There were no cell phones in 1968. But we were told that someone had called the police. We waited at least half an hour before the tall, basketball type police officer arrived on his immaculately kept motor bike. His arrival was timely in bringing a sense of calm to the gathering crowd.

Prior to his arrival, as we tried to reason with the driver of the laundry van, we quickly realized that he was working for a 'boss' who wouldn't be very pleased with what 'we' had done to his vehicle. He took no responsibility for the incident, insinuating that Bill should have stopped and allowed him to pull out onto the road. Minutes after the crash, people began to gather around us, a lot of people. We cautioned Bill to stop arguing with the driver and just wait for the police. After watching the crowd for ten minutes, seeing the number growing even bigger and not knowing when the police would arrive, I decided that this would be a good time to distribute our Gospel leaflets. Each one was the size of a regular A4 sheet of paper, explaining the story of salvation through brightly coloured illustrations of stories taken from the Bible; at the bottom of each sheet, there was a response slip, where a person could give their name and address and receive a free Bible correspondence course. A couple of us grabbed our Bibles and a handful of leaflets and started handing them to the ever growing circle of curious onlookers. Now the crowd was about a hundred strong, making a ring about thirty feet in diameter. Some were trying to stir up the crowd, shouting quick short phrases that we obviously didn't understand.

One of the people doing the inciting was a witchdoctor that I came face to face with. He looked at the sheets we were handing out, then yelled at the top of his voice and as he did, everyone immediately dropped the leaflets onto the ground. 'Now what do we do?' I thought. Not wanting to diminish the value of what we had be giving out, I bent down in front of each person and picked them up. Smiling at each person especially the children who I could see didn't want to drop their free pictures. The witchdoctor was enraged. His matted, mud caked, braided hair shaking along with the bones and other fetishes that hung around his neck, making it patently clear who and what he represented. It was fascinating to see this sad looking disheveled soul, commanding such authority in his ragged attire. Yet here he was, obviously seeing an opportunity to bring some home spun justice to bear in this world of unequal apartheid. He then began a sort of dance, along with a repetitive chant. Others joined in. We 'would be' evangelists, fresh off the boat from England now felt that we weren't amongst friends…And this was when the policeman arrived.

The incitement stopped. The driver of the van spoke with the Bantu officer. I tried to show him the marks on the road, which made it abundantly clear what had happened. He came right up to my face saying, "Are you trying to tell me my job?" To which I replied, "No sir". He then asked "Is your vehicle drivable?" Bill said "Yes". He said in a quiet voice, just loud enough for Bill and me to hear, "Then I suggest that you get into your car and drive away immediately". We did.

Bill had to get his car fixed, but we were all safe and thanking God that our encounters that day were all interesting, educational and relatively peaceful. Things could have turned out differently. All we can do is put our faith in God and leave the rest to Him. Elisabeth Elliot visited our church on one occasion to share her marvelous testimony, how her husband Jim had given his life at Shell Mera in the interior of Ecuador, in trying to reach the Auca Indians with the Gospel. Several missionaries were killed that day. And when Pauline commented that it was so sad for his life to be cut short and for him to die so young,

Elisabeth's reply was, "No, Jim had done what the Lord wanted him to do and He called him home, his assignment was complete". It's heartbreaking of course when loved ones are taken, but if we are able to accept that it is God and only God who is able to see the big picture, able to see the end from the beginning, then we would be able to enter into a peace, a healing mindset that really is always available to us as we put our trust in Christ. Another occasion, Pauline, Simon and I along with a friend Christine and our as yet unborn baby daughter Tracy, were almost wiped out as we turned a bend on a mountainous pass in the Eastern Transvaal of South Africa. I knew I didn't have much tread left on the tires but I was trying to keep up with the vehicle in front as we turned round a left hand bend. It was a sheer rock face on the left and a deep ravine on the right. Our car went into a skid on the dirt road, sliding rapidly towards the edge. Pauline and Christine shouted out "Jesus help us". As we were about to go over the edge, it's as though something or 'someone' literally pushed the car from the back. The car shot forward. Now it looked like we were going to smack into the rock face; I turned the steering wheel, the car grabbed and righted itself to continue along the road safely. I wasn't an experienced driver when this occurred, I had only been driving less than a year. The assignments that God had given us to do were obviously not yet finished.

1972 was the year we departed South Africa to serve the Lord in Papua New Guinea (see chapter 2). We lived in the capitol city of Port Moresby. Peter and Judy Wharton were living and working up in the hills of Sogeri 19 miles outside of the capitol. Peter was the headmaster of a local school and had begun the Gospel outreach ministry of 'Lifeline' from their home. The Bible correspondence study outreach was growing rapidly so it was agreed that for the convenience of following up on the 5,000 plus students, we would set up office in Port Moresby. It was also much easier to find volunteers to help with the marking and correcting of the scores of Bible studies returning to us each week.

During our time of working and serving in this, what was considered a primitive culture, P.N.G. did actually receive 'self-government', and then one year later 'independence'. It was a great time to be there. There was a fascinating sense of anticipation among the populous, most of whom were lovely, friendly people. Some however, bought into a rumoured belief that once independence arrived, so would all their 'Cargo'. Goods that had arrived by ship and air, always seemed to go to the 'expatriates'. The cargo cult believers felt that very soon, they would be entitled to receive it instead.

Petty crime was on the increase and it became necessary to be taking more precautions than previously. A new phenomenon had appeared, gangs. The car I was driving was a Datsun

SSS. The previous owner had installed an extremely loud horn that worked fine if just quickly pressed and released. But when pressed hard and long, it would emit this blood curdling scream which drew an inordinate amount of current from the battery. So much in fact that anything else using the battery would stop, such as the lights, radio and windshield wipers.

One evening just after sundown we were returning from our visit with the Wharton's on the mountain. The dirt road wound its way around lots of tight turns both left and right, with jungle on both sides. Then it straightened out for a long descent. About a hundred yards ahead we could see a group of men walking in the middle of the road. I slowed down. They didn't move. I gave a quick honk of the horn. They showed us that we were the ones that would have to stop. Pauline along with Simon and Tracy were in the car. Being fifty feet away from what I thought would be a nasty confrontation, I had a decision to make fast. It had become dark enough that I needed my headlights on so, still thirty feet from the mob, I initiated my 'secret weapon'. I accelerated and at the same time, pressed the horn as hard as I could. The mob had been looking at my headlights. Now my car 'disappeared' from sight yet let out this ear-piercing, unnatural scream!

Now, rather than a mob of about eight young ruffians standing in the road, blocking our path, bodies were flying left and right, feet and arms flailing about as the Datsun continued down the road. The lights came back on as soon as the horn went quiet. I never thought I'd be thanking the Lord for a wiring fault on my car, but I did that day and for many days following. And no, no-one was hit by the car. I share these stories, not to show disrespect to any of the countries that have opened their doors to us as a family, but to point out the reality that wherever you go, you can find people who have no respect for the rule of law. People who hold to a different set of rules and values. Those who follow Christ are not free to choose. He is 'the Standard'. His word is 'the guide book' for life, both for life here on earth and for eternal life with God. So believers in Christ in what He did for us on Calvary; paying the price of our debt of sin, that we might receive the free gift of salvation, being justified through the Blood of Jesus in the eyes of God, forgiven, just as if I'd never sinned, can't simply choose to sin and go on with a clear conscience. We belong to God. And we know that God is with us. He promised never to leave us nor forsake us. We just simply trust Him. We believe that what God said is true. That what God said is Truth. So we know by faith (which means trust), God will always be faithful to us.

This is the reason that Christians can't just do something that is contrary to God's Word. We can't do something that violates God's moral law such as kill, steal, and lie, commit adultery, and give our worship to another. We can't find a middle ground on abortion or same sex marriage – Why? Because

God's law doesn't change no matter what the progressive Supreme Court judges think or say. Society changes and we should all try to adapt and live in harmony together yes. But when society demands that we do something which brings us into conflict with God and with God's Word, no compromise can happen. Christian brothers and sisters, we all sin, but we have an understanding of the grace of God which He has made available to us through His Son Jesus. We serve a God of love and He will forgive us as we come to Him in sincere repentance regardless of the sins we have committed. But if we decide in the secret place of our heart, that we are going to do something in violation of God's word, then we move from under God's protection and go to the unprotected zone called 'rebellion'. This is where people live who have decided to live their life their way. But as for me and my house, we will serve the Lord. This doesn't mean that we won't have accidents, but it does mean that God is with me when I have the accident and He remains in control of the repercussions.

For instance; I had an accident in my truck in Guatemala as I was leaving the gated community where we lived in Guatemala City. It is an area where the upper class live, such as doctors, government workers and business people. Consequently it's one of the guarded areas where the children of these relatively well to do families, exhibit their latest toys to their friends. The divided road leading out of the area is 'one way' and is barely wide enough for passing a stationary vehicle. The speed limit is 25 km per hour. The 14 year old boy was sat astride his new 125cc motor cross track bike. He was enjoying showing off his new acquisition to his friends at the right side of the road; revving it in readiness to accelerate and go forward.

I was driving along on the left side of the road and to everyone's astonishment, the boy hung a left 'u' turn – right into my path as he accelerated away from his friends. I slammed my brakes on of course, but we collided at the same instance that he saw me. Thanks be to God that he had all the protective clothing on, as well as a helmet, because he bounced off the front of my truck and was quite dazed as he lay on the ground. His bike didn't do as well. It was firmly jammed underneath my F250 Heavy Duty diesel Crew cab. I 'happened' to have two doctors with me, who had come down with a team from our home church in Millwood's, Edmonton, Alberta. We ran to the boy and checked if he had anything broken. At first sight he seemed to be just dazed, so we helped him to the side of the road so that waiting traffic could get by us. Except that nobody was moving. This happened around 4.00 pm. A crowd gathered within minutes. The guard at the gate had already call the 'Bomberos'. In the Latin world of South and Central America, this simply means 'Fire and Ambulance'. They had also called the police. The transit police arrived first, but were quickly pushed aside by the Federal police. By this time, the father and older brother of the boy were on the scene. I was glad the police had arrived because the father was getting himself very agitated to the point of ripping my head off.

He was now very angry and expressing his hatred towards these 'gringos' who "Come down to his country just to rip the people off, then run back to their country". I was kneeling beside his son at the time and told him that "I'm not leaving, I'm staying here". Pauline and other missionaries had heard about what had happened and had come immediately, but the more they tried to reason with the father, the more out of control he was becoming. I asked Pauline and our friends to go home and pray that this turn of events would work out peacefully. As they were leaving, I caught sight of a neighbour who I knew to be a follower of the Lord. He was talking to the boy's older brother who now came and whispered to his father. Something happened at that moment. The father's rage ceased. It was as though someone had thrown a switch. The man now looked bewildered, conflicted and quiet. He sent the Bomberos away, carried his son to his Mercedes car and drove away. The son of another neighbour ran and got a jack to help me lift the truck off the motor cycle. All this time, we were still surrounded by crowds of people and of course, the police.

There is a rule in Guatemala and this is not a joke, it's true. If someone is hurt in an accident and the police are called, someone has to be arrested and held responsible. And looking around, it was pretty obvious who this person was going to be here. My license was taken from me and all my personal details recorded. The police then put the motor cycle on the back of my truck and assigned an officer to accompany me to the nearest police compound. On arrival I was placed in the corner of the processing shed. This is a large series of connected buildings the first of which houses the Commandant. He sits in the centre of the right hand side. He has a desk with an ancient looking typewriter in the middle. There are no other chairs nor furniture in the room, just a four foot white fluorescent light hanging from the ceiling. Before telling Pauline and our missionary friends to go home and pray, I asked them to please call my insurance agent to make sure he informed the company's lawyer about what had happened. I really wasn't sure what was going to happen to me next, all I did know was that I had to wait. I stood there, watching one after another being brought in and charged with different offences, being processed and escorted further into the chain of rooms beyond the far door. Hours went by. I was shaking following the accident but now, I was trembling from just standing on the spot for what was now four hours. All this time the Commandant had acted as though I was invisible. But, when the insurance lawyer walked in and spoke to him, he abruptly dismissed the lawyer as though he was a waste of time. Now there was two of us standing in the corner. The lawyer looking worried for his client, his client quietly asking his Lord to please intervene. I had heard many stories about the Guatemalan prison system. I had read the newspaper headlines of some of the atrocities that had been committed in the local jail. Much of the goings on within the jails of just about anywhere in Central America were actually run by the gangs who were in there for murder in the first place. So I knew that unless the Lord would intervene, I was in for a very unpleasant experience that could go on for some time. I also knew that if this was to happen, that too, was in His plan.

A few more minutes went by and in walked the father of the boy I had hit with my truck. I remember saying to myself, 'Oh no Lord. What's going to happen now?' He took one look at me and marched right over to the Commandant. A loud, what sounded to me like an argument ensued. The Commandant wasn't having any of it. He was used to shouting down any and all who got in his face. But the father of the boy didn't back down. Then the lawyer joined in. I didn't have a clue what was happening. They yelled at each other, until it seemed, they came to some kind of negotiated agreement. The lawyer and the father dashed out of the room. I was left standing there, again invisible. During all of this time, Pauline was at home, walking the floor, praying and crying out to the Lord. Wondering if she would ever see me again or whether she would be visiting me in the infamous jail in the city. Much prayer was offered up that night, not just from her and our missionary friends but also from the Millwood's team from our home church in Edmonton, who were there working on the construction of the school.

Another hour of silent prayer went by from me. Then about 9:00 pm, the father of the boy along with the lawyer came almost running back into the police chief's office. The conversation now was quieter and shorter. The Commandant looked over the sheet of paper they had brought to him and eventually he nodded, got out of his seat and allowed the lawyer to sit at his typewriter and between the three of them, typed what turned out to be an Affidavit, spelling out the event of the day and declaring the police department free of any culpability. The paper was pulled from the machine and for the first time they looked over at me and explained that in order for me not to have to go into the prison system, the lawyer, the father and I had to sign this affidavit. I quickly signed it, as did they. The father then explained that the police chief couldn't let me go earlier because the boy had to go to hospital. The previous argument had been to accept a letter from the doctor saying that the boy was fine. The affidavit was to clear the Commandant of any further responsibility in the boy's case. From the moment the son had spoken to the father, the father had been working on my behalf to set me free. What a marvellous illustration.

The father had been told by people who saw the accident as well as from the boy himself that it was not my fault and I should at all costs be prevented from being imprisoned. I later was informed that one of our neighbor's asked the father if he knew who we were that we were missionaries coming to help their young people, building a technical school to better equip the marginalized young adults of Guatemala. This was at the point when as previously mentioned, everything seemed to change. I thanked the father and the lawyer for going to such great lengths in getting the necessary letter from the doctor in order to save me from jail. The father then told me that they are also followers of the Lord. We joined together and gave thanks to God for His goodness, mercy and faithfulness to us all.

Boy was I glad to get home that night, getting a 'royal welcome' from Pauline and an extra special hug.

The next day, I was able to rejoin the work team as they continued on the task of building the William Cornelius Vocational Training Centre.

God was about to open the windows of heaven......

CHAPTER 6

GOD'S SUPPLY LINES

Remember the magpie knocking on the tree? Then came the message; "Just keep on knocking, the stuff's in there". Followed by the message; "Do you see those cows? I own the cattle on a thousand hills and the wealth in every mine belongs to Me!" I knew that God's store houses were full and I knew that we didn't have any money in the account to go blindly building a one to two million dollar technical school, Christian or otherwise. I also knew that it did not sit right in my heart going round asking men and women for money, which is what was suggested I do. Others advised me to go to the bank and take out a mortgage loan in faith. I said that I would rather trust God to provide the money up front so that there would be no debt.

So, knowing that God would have us to just keep on knocking and believing that God owns everything in the world anyway, we produced a 'Projects within the Project' booklet, listing each building phase requirements which was then further broken down into areas of priority. This was then itemized in detail complete with rounded off pricings. When anyone wanted to know the cost of any part of the project, we would simply give them or send them a copy of the project booklet. We covered this in prayer, making a firm commitment in faith, that we would never spend money that we didn't already have in the bank. Some thought this to be impractical and counter-productive, especially when we were in the middle of a building phase. But we held firm to the principle in order to prove to ourselves that putting our faith purposefully in God's faithfulness was enough. It did mean that on two really difficult occasions we had to stop the work and lay off our national workers. We don't really know why this had to happen. I've given it a lot of thought and think that perhaps God was actually testing our resolve.

On these occasions, all workers were paid their wages and benefits and all bills were paid. We had no debt. These were the two anomalies that interrupted the steady flow of activity that began immediately following the long awaited permit from the Ministry of Education.

We got official word on the 20th September, 2000 that we could start to build the W.C.V.T.C. (Though it would take another 2 years before the land was signed over to us – 'usufructo').

Two months later we finally received the full set of drawings from the Guatemalan company who had been hired to translate the E.M.I. drawings into local codes and legal jargon. At last, we were ready to begin. Fasting and prayer continued on a regular basis but the bureaucratic run around was over. We were now able to concentrate on the planning for visiting work teams. Thanks to Don Raymer and Gillian Rumney of the E.R.D.O. department of the P.A.O.C. we were included on a list of options given the P.A.O.C. churches who were looking for a 'short term' project. One that their missions committee could present to their congregations and Board members. Now we began receiving enquiries as to what our requirements would be of a team coming down from Canada: What would be our expectations of them? What should they bring? How much money? How many people allowed on a team? Are there any age limits? On and on it went. It was also suggested by the E.R.D.O. desk that each team bring $5,000.00 for each work week that they were on site, to contribute towards the building materials. This money would typically be sent down several weeks before the arrival of the team, in order for us to have the materials on site ready to be used. Most teams would come for two weeks, which helped enormously towards building materials. We received 6 to 8 teams each year, during the building period from the year 2000 to 2008. Pauline was constantly busy communicating with churches across Canada, organizing the team's accommodation, meals and transport. Our snack coordinator always made sure the team members were looking forward to snack time. The worksite supervisor kept the job list up to date so that the teams could get right to work as soon as the morning devotions were over. I played the part of the general gopher. Making sure the team members had all the materials and tools they needed to get the job done. Quite often we were blessed with extra E.M.I. engineers who were perhaps between projects or just visiting Guatemala. Whatever the reason, there was always some challenging aspect of the project that would keep them busy. We truly thank the Lord for His love and grace in sending all these professional people, to give of their time and experience to the furtherance of His kingdom.

Let me pause and take you back to..........

3:00 pm 9th July, 1996 when the Executive members of the Assemblies of God of Guatemala, joined Pastor Sazo, two staff members from P.I.E.D.A.D. office (Child Care sponsorship office) and Pauline and I, as we marched around the piece of derelict land and claimed it for God, His Kingdom and the William Cornelius Vocational Training Centre. We tramped through the piles of garbage, weeds and rocks stating in faith that this property would soon accommodate a beautiful school, where young, marginalized Guatemalan youth, would not only learn a trade but would have the opportunity of hearing the

Gospel and learning what it means to be a follower of Christ. After marching round the perimeter, we stood in a circle in the middle and worshiped God, giving Him all the glory for what He would do on this piece of land.

One of the main purposes of this book is to give real life examples of how faithful is our loving heavenly Father. How often do we hear young people today lamenting that, 'we don't see God working miracles these days' As though God has gone quiet or has changed His ways of doing things. God is just as active and involved in His world and in His people's lives today as He has ever been. But, in order to see His hand and witness His moving in the affairs of men and women, we need to be exercising faith. Faith (trusting in God) is the currency of heaven being used here on earth. In the book of Genesis we see various instances where God spoke to Abram, later called Abraham and actually told Abram what He wanted him to do. His instructions came complete with promises. And when Abram requested some basic clarification (see Genesis 15:2) God lovingly took him outside and gave him a night sky illustration of how numerous would be his offspring (Gen. 15:5) And Genesis 15:6 says: 'And he believed in the Lord, and He accounted it to him for righteousness'.

Faith is faith. Whether exercised in the Old Testament through obedience to God, or exercised in the New Testament, through the grace of our Lord Jesus Christ, it is made available to us by the finished work of the Cross. Throughout the Gospels we see what it was that Jesus was looking for in the lives of the people He healed. (See Matthew 8 10-13, 9:2, 22, 28-29). The Lord is still looking for and expects His followers to speak, live and act in a manner that shows that we trust Him.

When we speak a word of faith in agreement with God's Word and His Kingdom principles, God sees our faith in action and is able to respond to it.

If on the other hand, we have become convinced that God isn't working miracles anymore, or even answering prayer, which in itself is a miracle, then whatever grade of prayer life we have become comfortable with, has a direct relationship to the level of divine action. In other words, if God's gracious hand is only moved through prayer, what will God do if we don't pray?

Here is an example of a prayer of faith prayed on our behalf on the 15th May, 2000 in response to a news update 'Memo' that Pauline and I sent out requesting prayer over our local team, in view of some challenges that we were facing at the time, we wrote: 'Pray that each one will sense an anointing of faith, wisdom and power as they rise each day'. Zendra and Dr. Gary Manley attached this prayer to their e-mail:

"I pray that powers, principalities, rulers & authorities be bound over you and Alan and the project

for the land and development. And loose the angels of heaven and the waring angels to be posted all round about you, that the will of God be completed this day! That every desire of your heart be granted.

I ask You Lord God to send Your Word this day to release the funds for this project, you are not a God of lack but a God of plenty and Your arm is not too short to fulfill the needs of Alan and Pauline for this project. So in the Name of Jesus, I call the project into being, I call this land into perfect alignment for Your namesake and I ask You Lord God to give Pauline and Alan favour with all they come into contact with regarding the land. We bless Your name Lord God of Abraham, Isaac and Israel. Amen".

Love to you both Zendra and Gary.

Now I'm sure that some of you who are reading this will be feeling uncomfortable with the seeming boldness of this type of faith stating prayer. Yet nothing you see here violates scripture. In fact, it lines up most appropriately with the Biblical narrative, see:

1 Sam. 1:17, 1 Sam. 17:45-47. Acts 9:32-35. Phil 4:19.

Jesus repeated several times that we are to come to the Father and ask for that which we desire and it shall be done. John 14:12-14, 15: 7-8. Of course our request must reflect our standing in Christ as we abide in Him. God will not answer a prayer in the affirmative if what we are asking does not agree with His will and purpose.

These issues of faith and the functioning of the gifts and fruits of the Holy Spirit have historically brought division to the Church. But it is time for us to put our petty differences aside and focus on the unity of the Body, allowing the unifying work of the Holy Spirit, who knows those who are His, to bless us as we give our attention to the work of building God's Kingdom, not ours. Denominations are good only as long as they are bringing glory to God and are being used of God for the growing of His Kingdom. Once a church denomination becomes focused only on its 'history' or its 'traditions' and is comfortable with its progressive identity, no longer seeing its primary objective as a Gospel lighthouse, then its usefulness to God is over. Yet a smoking flax the Lord will never snuff out. Revival is always possible, but requires faith and the prayers of the faithful.

Around about the time we received Gary and Zendra's prayer attached to an e-mail, we also received a financial gift from an anonymous donor. This was so timely as the department of education lawyer had recently warned us to try to put up a fence as soon as possible, the reason being, once squatters settle in, they are hard to evict. So we commenced on the fence immediately as well as building a 'garita', a guard house which at that time we used as an office. It also brought great relief in another way; up until now we had to go to the business next door whenever we needed to use the bathroom. Now we had everyday relief both for ourselves and for our volunteer work team members.

We couldn't know it at the time, only God knows what's coming and when, and He really isn't telling us anything up front other than what He has already given to us in His Word; but following that first donation, we were going to be busy pretty much constantly for the next eight years. As I have explained already there were two or three periods of time when not a lot was happening on the building but even at these times there was always research and planning going on for the eventual startup of the school.

Beginning in the year 2000, the following events took place. Some were happening simultaneously but most occurred consecutively. None of them could have happened without God's intervention and provision. Following the soil study and the building contractor's strong suggestion, we realized that in order to save money on the pouring of the fifty nine huge footings, it would be necessary to remove a meter and a half off the whole area of the property, due to it being a landfill. We made the need known that this initial step was going to cost $10,000.00. We prayed and asked the Lord to supply this needed finance and very soon we received the money in the bank and were able to begin this huge messy job.

Our building contactor was a well know Christian man who understood our need to approach this great work in phases. As a man of faith himself, he knew we were trusting God for His provision and that we would not be going to the bank to ask for a loan. We agreed in principle to tackle the building of the 55,000 square foot structure in three general phases; floors 1, 2 and 3. The ground floor includes over fifty deep, massive footings, each one having a two foot square concrete column rising up to the level of the second floor. All reinforced with many lengths of one inch steel rebar which were further reinforced with rings of ½ inch steel rebar, all coming out of the ground, pointing as it were their worship up to the God of all creation. Between each column ran a horizontal grid of more of these enormous cages of steel which after being boxed in, were filled with high grade concrete. We were not building on sand by any means but the structure needed to be designed to the highest standards in order to withstand the many tremours that are a regular occurrence in this geographic area.

The estimated cost that we agreed to for phase one was Can. $133,058.73. At the time of signing the contract we had less than half that amount in the bank so we told the contractor to please hold off starting the work until all the money for phase 1 was procured.

We assured him that we would fast and pray and trust the Lord to send the finances needed at the right time so that he could work phase by phase. The money needed to cover the cost of phase one arrived on time and we were able to pay the full amount to finish this huge phase.

As you read this chapter it would be easy to get the wrong impression that the Slaters could fast and pray and get whatever they asked for. Once again let me reiterate, this story is not about us, it's about God giving us an assignment to do for His glory and for His kingdom purposes. It was our part along with the local team, to carefully keep our eyes fixed on the Lord, as we each gave leadership to the hundreds of volunteers who came down to give of their time, talent and treasure, all simply in obedience to the Master. We each played a part in making the need known in arranging and attending meetings, phoning contacts, chasing paperwork, planning volunteer work teams, giving expert and professional construction advice, drawing plans complete with calculations, showing how to mix concrete and lay cement blocks. Contacting churches arranging services, hosting work teams, buying materials, giving leadership to national workers and doing it all in English and Spanish.

The Lord Jesus, God the Son is our Master. We just follow His instructions. The Holy Scriptures not only tell us how to live, they are replete with promises and principles that if we were to follow with all our heart, we could be assured that the things we would be asking God for, would be things in accordance with His will and purpose. For instance, in Deuteronomy 23 v 9, God is graciously telling His people up front, how they can be sure to remain under the covering of His protection and blessing. It says:

'When the army goes out against your enemies,
then keep yourself from every wicked thing'

This is a terrific lesson for all today in our present world of compromise and complacency. God's Holiness and righteousness is just the same in this day of grace today, as it was in Old Testament times when God's people lived under the law. And although we are not under the law but under grace through the work of the Cross, if we want God to answer our prayers if we want to experience the manifest presence of God in our lives, we need to keep ourselves clean, not only in our bodies but also in our hearts. For this verse is saying – 'When you are doing something for God if you want Him to grant you His help and favour, keep yourself pure'. God can't help us if we are entertaining unclean things in our lives. Thanks be to God for His grace and mercy, but we must be sincere in our humility as we ask Him for forgiveness of our sins. Once our hearts are clean from wicked and impure rebellion and disobedience, then are we free to come into His presence only through the cleansing power of the Blood of Jesus. Am I suggesting that we need to be perfect in order to come to God? No I'm not for none of us are. But I am strongly suggesting that for us to live in the victory that is ours through Christ, we must keep our sins and short comings on a short leash. When we sin knowingly, run to God to seek His forgiveness, don't do the usual in running away from God to hide. This gives Satan an opportunity to give you another shot in the solar plexus and keep you on the run. Living a life style of humility and confession, keeps the enemy away and brings us spiritual confidence. This helps us maintain victorious equilibrium because a daily routine of spiritual cleansing before the Lord, deals not only with our sins of commission but also the carnal actions, words and thoughts we permit ourselves to have that are just as offensive to God, but due to our spiritual immaturity we don't even realize it. Spiritual warfare demands our personal consecration and sanctification.

Once we had the full set of design drawings for the whole of the building project, the first order of business for the visiting work teams were the perimeter walls. There was a constant need to be vigilant as we were to learn one morning on our arrival at the land ready to get to work. We had borrowed the cement mixer from the mission office of Child Care Plus as well as purchasing one for the school building needs.

Both machines were covered by tarps to protect them from the rain. You can imagine our surprise when we pulled the tarps off to find the two Briggs and Stratton engines gone! We did have a guard living on the property but that didn't prevent the robbers from carefully cutting a hole through the chain link fence, quietly dismantling the two engines and disappearing into the night.

While different sections of the surrounding high wall were being built, our project engineer and worksite supervisor kept the volunteer work teams busy, working on the construction of a two story apartment building in the North-West corner of the property. Immediately following this, the contractor marked out first, the position of the multi-purpose hall, followed by the positioning of those massive footings mentioned earlier.

We were blessed with many volunteer teams who were always ready and willing to do whatever they were asked to do. We knew that each team would contribute a donation from their church to help with the purchase of the building materials. It was great to be able to keep them busy with these separate buildings from the main school building at that time. Our prayer requests were still going heavenward, not only for work teams but also for divine provision in regard to the financing of the building contract for the school. The multipurpose hall was being built simultaneously with the first phase of the school.

We actually broke ground for the multipurpose hall in the January, 2003 and God was so wonderfully faithful to us in providing the funds for phase 1 as mentioned so that work could begin on this great building project in the February of 2003.

It would still take several months before all the official paperwork was signed and sealed but at least, now we were able to get started on the building. There was a six month pause between the finances coming in for the first phase and the miracle provision of finances for the second. If we as the local planning team would have been able to see into the future and see what God was doing and what He was going to do, it would have been so much easier on our nerves and on our ability to patiently wait. There were occasions along the way in this process when I knew that God was telling us to wait. No, we didn't have the pillar of smoke by day and pillar of fire by night, but we did have the 'Comforter-Counsellor' giving us guidance, though we weren't always able to hear His still small voice.

The estimated cost of phase 2 was Can. $205,246.29. Much prayer was being offered up as we sought the face of God, but we had no natural source of funding for such a large amount. Phase 2 was more expensive than phase1 because it included the fabrication of many reinforced concrete beams on top of which was poured a reinforced concrete floor of 1,540 square meters. Weeks would go by and while we did enjoy seeing the multipurpose hall slowly being erected, being built by our visiting volunteer work teams under the leadership of our worksite supervisor, it was challenging to our faith to be constantly seeing the 59 columns standing fifteen feet out of the ground, like some giant, petrified forest. We just kept on believing that God knew what He was doing even if we didn't. We had lots of people coming through Guatemala who had heard about the William Cornelius Vocational Training Centre project and indicated that they would like to visit and see the worksite. We enjoyed showing such visitors around and would go out of our way to do so.

Early November 2003 we received an e-mail from a pastor in British Columbia informing us that he and his father were coming to Guatemala for a preaching engagement and would love to come and visit the worksite while in country. The very informal tour took place on Tuesday 25th November 2003. Pauline walked around with several of the group that came, whilst I gave a detailed description to pastor Derrick what the school would do for the underprivileged youth, who would one day soon, be attending this unique place. As they were about to leave to go back to their accommodation, I mentioned that Pauline and I would be coming back to Canada soon on furlough. Pastor Derrick suggested that perhaps we could come speak at his church in West Kelowna. I replied saying we could arrange that as we would be speaking at the German Pentecostal Church in Kelowna. He asked me why I, an Englishman, would be speaking at the German Mission Link Churches. I explained that we were on the pastoral staff at the Mill Woods Pentecostal Church at the time of my ordination and that we were receiving much of our support as missionaries through the Mission Link Churches. His face lit up! "Now I know why I had to come to Guatemala". He went on to explain that a committee had the task of finding where a donation could be placed that would reflect the strong German Branch missionary vision, following the recent sale of the Kelowna German Pentecostal Church! He asked me to prepare a letter describing the challenge we faced with phase 2 of the project. I delivered the letter to him at the airport the following morning. We sought the throne of God as we fasted, prayed and waited.

It was five days later that we received an e-mail from Pastor Derrick informing us that the decision had been made to send a cheque to the P.A.O.C. World Missions Department in the sum of Can. $205,246.29 designated for the building of phase 2 –W.C.V.T.C. Joyful tears were plentiful. Pauline screamed so loud, I commented later that I wouldn't be surprised if they had heard it in Kelowna!

God's timing is always perfect, even during those times when we have to wait.

Pauline and Edna were so charged by this, they committed to fast and pray together, seeking the Lord to provide the funds required in order for the building contractor to be able to continue on and complete the third floor of the school. Their prayer was to the effect that the money would be put into the bank account, prior to our leaving to go on furlough. Apparently 12 weeks was plenty of time for God to answer their prayer. The funds were in the bank before we left Guatemala at the beginning of March 2004. We traversed across Canada, reporting back to our supporting churches over the next seven month, returning to Guatemala the first week of October.

Try to imagine our thrill and astonishment as we now walked on to the property. The concrete structure was essentially complete. There were lots of areas where walls still had to be built but as our highly skilled, worksite supervisor showed us around, we were overcome with joy. Pauline cried as we caught our first glimpse of the majestic staircase rising through the middle of the central courtyard area. The supervisor (who wished to remain anonymous) had done an absolutely magnificent job while we were away. Both he and our E.M.I. engineer, along with their team of very able national workers, had faithfully and passionately served the Lord, applying their gifting's and energy to this great undertaking. We truly thank the Lord for His obvious calling on their lives, that they would leave home and family for this five year period in order to serve Him in such a blessed and practical way, for the sake of the myriad, worthy young people of Guatemala, many from the poorer sectors of the metropolis of Guatemala and surrounding area. We do have some wonderful stories of how lives and families have been changed by the new opportunities that have been provided by the existence of the W.C.V.T.C. But this must wait for a later chapter.

Huge donations as well as many smaller ones, had arrived toward the building of this great structure. Quite a number of these gifts to the work of God were anonymous. We have no idea where they came from except that they were prompted by the precious Holy Spirit. It was during this period of time that we began to realize that something extraordinary was happening. We had come to accept the process of making the need known, followed by a waiting period, then getting the good news usually through the E.R.D.O. office that money had been received and was now on its way to our bank. We never had more than was immediately needed but we, as a local planning team would prioritize the list of jobs waiting to be done, the money always seemed to be arriving just at the right time. There were a couple of times when we got a little ahead of ourselves and were unable to keep our national workers, but in general, the progress of finishing off the building was kept going through the financial donations that were provided by the stream of volunteer teams coming down from our Pentecostal Assemblies of Canada churches, from the many parts of our wonderful country. Also, several teams from the States came and worked and gave of their time and gifting's. It was truly a time of the ongoing testing of our faith. And in the testing of our faith, we were able to see the hand of God working on our behalf. God was showing us that when He makes a promise: "I will provide everything you need to complete the work" (Chapter 3) He means what He says and He is faithful to always keep His word.

So now we had the guard house built, the apartment/office built and the multipurpose building almost finished. The building contractor had finished the foundations, columns and beams as well as the second and third floors.

The worksite supervisor and the engineers were constantly requesting the funds to purchase cement, sand, re-bar, cement blocks and wooden planks for building the forms, in order to keep our national and volunteer workers busy from 2002 through 2006.

Each month, we would send out a memo to our friends and supporting churches and ex-team members, giving everyone an update on the progress of the W.C.V.T.C. project. It would begin with words of praise and thanksgiving to the Lord for His grace and faithfulness in the way He was pouring out His blessings upon what we were doing. Then it included information as to the immediate needs we had with the building schedule. Making the needs known was the wisdom of God, for it spared us the crass embarrassment of having to ask for money, while giving a would be donor the freedom to volunteer his or her help without the embarrassing pressure. Most of all, it allowed the blessed Holy Spirit to be the 'go-between Agent' throughout this whole process. Not everyone involved, agreed with this method of fund raising but it seemed to be the most appropriate way of getting the job done without interfering with what God was doing.

During the building years, the list of jobs and projects within this great project seemed to be getting longer rather than shorter. The closer we got to finish the structure, the more we realized how many things still needed to be done. In chapter seven we will review a further chain of miracles as we see God's hand outstretched on our behalf providing for the needs encountered as we proceeded through the finishing off process.

CHAPTER 7

THE MIRACULOUS CHECK-OFF LIST.

O nce the structure was nearing completion and our worksite supervisor was filling in the walls with the help of our national workers and capable volunteer workers from Canada, we turned our attention to such things as roll doors, regular doors, windows, electrical fittings, and plumbing equipment and floor and roof coverings. Each of these items we knew would cost many thousands of dollars. Yet we were constantly aware of the promise of God, spoken through Paul in his New Testament letter to the believers in Philippi, chapter 4 and verses 19 & 20 where he says; 'And my God shall supply all your need according to His riches in glory by Christ Jesus. Now to our God and Father be glory forever and ever. Amen'.

The promise we had received prophetically several years earlier at the El Shaddai church, where the Lord assured us that He would provide everything we needed to complete the work, was never far from our minds. We simply trusted in God's faithfulness in keeping His word.

Events from years ago in South Africa we now realize, were key to giving us the determined resilience needed at this juncture in time, when it would have been so easy to throw in the towel and lose the vision altogether. 1967 We were young, married only two years with a 4 month old baby, Simon. Living in a new country, new culture, and new job. The new house went with the job, with the mortgage payment being taken out of my salary each month, leaving us with only enough for food and nothing left over for furniture. As we bought furniture, it came out of the food money. It was during this time that we really began to see the hand of God helping us in the midst of our need. Pauline was learning how to shop for food in a very creative manner. Buying over-ripe tomatoes at giveaway prices meant that we ate boiled, fried, grilled and raw tomatoes for the fourth week of one particular month. South Africa was still in the throes of apartheid at that time, but there was no shyness on Pauline's part on lining up with our African friends, to buy half a loaf of bread or a bottle of milk every day because we had no fridge. We were able to do it over a period of months. Simon never went hungry as we always made sure he had lots of formula. But there wasn't much food in the house when the fridge was delivered. I'll never forget the almost uncontrolled glee in Pauline's voice and face when I came home from work that day. Apparently, we were the 1,000[th] customer to purchase one of these fridges; when it was delivered, it arrived stocked full with Del Monte food! We praised and thanked the Lord greatly for His timely goodness to us.

Several months later we needed to purchase another article of furniture, but once again, this meant the food would deplete well before my next pay cheque. I was sat at break time and was reading a small book of scriptures. The page had opened to the 'Sermon on the Mount', my eyes dropped onto the portion in Matthew 6; 25-27 which says: "Therefore I say to you, do no worry about your life, what you will eat or what you drink; nor about your body, what you will put on. Is not life more than food and the body more than clothing. Look at the birds of the air, for they neither sow nor reap nor gather into barns; yet your heavenly Father feeds them. Are you not of more value than they? Which of you by worrying can add one cubit to his stature..." I read further where Jesus put it all into proper perspective with saying:

"…….But seek first the Kingdom of God and His righteousness, and all these things shall be added to you……"

I knew in my spirit that God had quickened these verses to me in a special way and that He was confirming His help toward us. I thanked Him for speaking to me through the Holy Spirit and returned to my workplace, knowing with assurance that all would be well. Later in the afternoon, as I walked up the driveway to our home, Pauline opened the door and shouted, "Guess what?"

"I know!" I yelled back.

"What?"

"We have food".

"How do you know?"

"The Lord told me today at break time". I replied.

Yes our driveway was long! We were now laughing and crying as Pauline explained what had happened. Earlier in the day, Ruth, our neighbour, came to ask Pauline if we could use a week's supply of groceries; unbeknown to her husband Michael, Ruth had already done her grocery shopping. He too had bought groceries. So there they were with double groceries for a family of six! As you can imagine Pauline did not hesitate in her response, we were only too happy to help out in this way! God's ways are far better and way beyond our worrying and certainly beyond our planning.

These early years in South Africa were stretching for both Pauline and me, but in different ways. I had to do the manly thing like go off to work each day and the times when we were invited to different church events, I was expected to be ready to speak from God's Word. But Pauline's routine was tougher because she had to fill her days with the mundane things of being a young mum in a different culture. Walking everywhere, pushing Simon in his pram as we had no vehicle. Having to wash by hand his soiled nappies, due to the fact we had no washing machine. Spending most days with no-one to talk to as we lived so far away from any of the people we knew.

Young readers wouldn't know this, but during those years of apartheid, even when the rest of the world was watching Neil Armstrong stepping onto the moon, South Africa had no television! We had radio and land line telephones, but that was it.

It was less than a year later that we had the wonderful news – we were expecting our second child. Tracy burst onto the scene on the 9th August, 1968. I had the joy of being there for her birth, giving Simon his best friend and companion through his growing years as well as doubling the number of nappies needing to be washed!

Throughout those initial years of marriage when even under ideal circumstances, nerves can get a little raw, Pauline and I clung tightly to the strong relationship we had with the Lord Jesus and this would help us find our way through some extraordinary times of stress that came our way. Grace would shine through our arguments. Mercy would win out through our silent-treatment times. Love always broke our stubborn wills, to bring peace and joy back to our growing family. It was the unshakeable love we both had for Jesus that would always steady the ship, even in the roughest storm. We were learning over and over again that we could always trust in God's faithfulness to us. How could we not show our faithfulness back to Him through the love and faithfulness we truly felt in our love for one-another?

All was settling down well and our ministry on the township of Tembisa, just outside Johannesburg was being well received. Yet as our second year became a thing of the past, we both began to sense a strong desire to pick up and move to the town of Nelspruit in the Eastern Transvaal. The obvious attraction that many of our friends considered we were feeling, was that Nelspruit was the place where the Emmanuel Press was situated. Emmanuel Press was effectively the central ministry office for all the British Assemblies of God 'Lifeliners'; the team of young people who worked during the day in our own trades and professions, while serving the Lord in our spare time. This was the place where Gospel literature was printed and distributed throughout South Africa as well as many other African countries beyond. Each piece of Gospel literature had within it an invitation slip, for anyone reading who had the desire, to receive the Lord Jesus Christ into their heart. This could then be returned to the Emmanuel Press office in order to receive a free Bible study series, lesson by lesson, helping the new follower of Christ to grow in their faith.

It's true that being in Nelspruit was a nice thought because it is such a beautiful place, but this was not what was driving these desires. We both just knew that this was what God wanted us to do. So in spite of the many who advised to the contrary, we made the move. It wasn't easy starting again, but we knew that we made the move in the will of God. Much went against us in this decision, but this just strengthened our resolve that with God's help, all would work out well.

Finding work was not difficult but wages in the country towns were much less than in the big city. Finding a place to live was a bigger challenge.

First, we went to live in a missionary's home at Kaapmuiden, situated 25 miles East of Nelspruit, not too far from the Mozambique border. It was located up in the low lying hills of this semi-tropical farmland, about one kilometer off the highway. The only neighbours we had were dotted occasionally along the dirt road dividing one farm from another. We were warned not to go wandering into the fields as there could be rats and snakes and the occasional troop of monkeys. The crops were high and lush, mainly sugar cane and corn but there were also some wonderful flame trees and jacaranda trees in the area. Driving through this beautiful part of what the locals called 'God's own country', one couldn't avoid drinking in the delightful smell of orange blossom that permeates the atmosphere for several months of the year.

The missionaries were on furlough at the time, back in England, returning to South Africa several months later. This allowed us time to look around, for a suitable place to rent that would suit our budget. My take home pay was R50.00 per week, which was the equivalent of $50.00. In light of this we were praying and asking the Lord to guide us in the right direction to something really reasonable.

Travelling to work and back each day in the old clonker that we had, soon proved to be too much, as I pulled into our driveway one evening with clouds of blue smoke bellowing out of the exhaust pipe. Thumbing to work and back certainly lengthened my work day but it did two other things also; I spent a lot more time in prayer as I was walking along the road and I learned to really appreciate the grace and patience of the African folk who I would meet along the way. Most were truly friendly, often stopping to ask me if I wanted a ride and helping in any way they could. I will always be grateful and thankful for these acts of kindness shown to me in spite of the rough treatment and cruelty I often witnessed toward the Bantu people from the whites.

One memory of our stay at the Kaapmuiden house stands out quite vividly. It was one Saturday morning. Pauline was preparing lunch in the kitchen, Tracy was still tiny, sitting in her carry-cot, while Simon was playing out on the back step. I was relaxing in the bathtub, not having to thumb a ride this day, when Pauline let out this blood curdling scream, shouting my name at the top of her voice, which I understood quite clearly meant- 'Come at once, this is urgent!' I leapt out of the bath, grabbing a towel in order to maintain as much dignity as possible and ran as fast as I could in the direction of the commotion. Simon had ventured a wee bit further from the step and was playing in the dirt, when he came to tell us that he had seen something out there. It was a snake! I grabbed the nearest thing to hand, which was an axe; with the other hand still holding on tight to the towel I charged out like St. George intent on slaying this ten foot would-be dragon. With all the noise and vibrating action going on, the snake had gone off to hide under a barrel. I bravely lopped off a chunk of its tail. Then as I pushed the barrel over the snake reared its head, ready to bite its foe. So I dropped the axe and grabbed the garden hoe and finished it off with one swift blow. This, what only turned out to be a three foot snake, had obviously just swallowed a frog or a rat and was looking for a quiet place to digest its dinner. It should never have picked our backyard. And, you've guessed it, my bath water was cold by the time I returned from the battle.

The double challenge before us now was getting the car repaired along with finding a place to live in Nelspruit. Wherever we have lived throughout our travels we have always found God's ever present help in times of need, actually presenting itself to us through His wonderful family that we call 'the Church'.

One Sunday morning we were chatting with a Dutch missionary, Ralph. He wanted to know what was happening with our car. I told him it had probably blown a piston or a valve or even worse but that I couldn't afford to have it repaired yet, until life settled down into a routine. He said, "Don't worry, my son is a mechanic and he'll fix it in his spare time for just the cost of parts". God is so good! At this time we were told about a cottage on the outskirts of Nelspruit that we could look at. The rent was R50.00 per month, but was rudimentary in regard to facilities. It was the right price, so we moved in as soon as the car was fixed. Living in this cottage was......interesting. It did have a bathroom, but to have hot water, I had to chop firewood and build a fire under a steel drum. There was no electricity coming to the house, so we used a variety of oil lamps, which Pauline thought was romantic. We actually enjoyed using them, getting used to them after a while. The kitchen consisted of a sink and a two ring Calorgas type unit which sat next to the sink, no oven. The cottage was basically a fifteen by thirty foot box with walls for the toilet and the two bedrooms. But for the months that we were living there it was home. Simon was now 2.1/2 years old and Tracy going into her first year.

We were satisfied with our situation and began to put feelers out as to what we could do as far as ministry was concerned. We attended the Nelspruit Assemblies of God Church, when we weren't taking services out at the plantations and villages. What a thrill it was for Pauline and me to be going by invitation to the many little village churches, along with the children, in the footsteps of Austin and Ingrid Chawner and Hubert and Jean Phillips, pioneer missionaries of Mozambique and the Eastern Transvaal of South Africa. Once again we found the people to be loving, kind and welcoming to these young, English self-supporting missionaries with funny accents.

As always I was working full time as a machinist in one of the local machine shops. A major bonus when working in a farming area as well as in a central town for maintenance in the forestry industry, is that you learn a whole new set of skills and abilities to add to what you already have in your toolbox.

I learned how to weld, which is usually unheard of due to union restrictions. I repaired broken gears for the presses of Emmanuel Press. I learned the art of putting Heli coils in cylinder heads of Mercedes Benz in such a way as to render it unnecessary to remove the cylinder head. And I learned how to re-metal babbet- white metal bearings as well as the skill of crankshaft grinding and engine reboring. Why am I telling you all this? Because even though I was a fully qualified machinist in Great Britain, I would need all these new skills in the not too distant future as we continued on our journey from country to country. Even in such unforeseen things as these, God is faithful!

Still in Nelspruit and settled into our rented 'box cabin' we were invited to visit a confectionery shop where new friends from the church were making cakes, pies and pastries. The wife and daughter were running the shop. The husband managed one of the large saw mills out in the neighbouring town of White River. After work one evening, Pauline and I along with the kids made our way over to the cake shop. The mother and daughter team had a double barrel treat in store for us. After giving us a guided tour of their new bakery, they loaded us up with cakes, pies and other pastries that would rival any confectionary competition. But, as we were preparing to leave, the husband, who I hadn't met before, suddenly appeared and said, "Well, is there something you want to ask me?" I had no idea what he was talking about and I replied, "No". What the husband and I didn't know was that Pauline in prior discussion with this loving mother and daughter, duo, May and Dawn, were planning to get their two innocently ignorant men together in order for me to enquire about a vacant house the husband owned. But I was completely in the dark about it. So, long story short, he offered to let us live in this house that he owned for the same rent we were paying for the box-cottage. Pauline and I drove over to have a look to see whether or not we wanted to make the move. We checked and double checked to see if we were at the correct address. There were just three, spaciously detached, brick houses in their own cul-de-sac which we found out later, our friend owned, him and his family living in the first one. They were beautifully positioned overlooking the town of Nelspruit with the majestic hills of White River, in the distance. There was a huge, several acre open field in front of the house and a koppie, which is Afrikaans for Small Mountain, at the rear,

It was surrounded by gorgeous flowering trees and bushes and at the back of the house were several huge trees laden down with big green, shiny fruits, that later we were to discover were mangos. To us, this house, sitting right in the middle, was a mansion. Three bedrooms, dining room, kitchen, living room and bathroom. That night we gave thanks to our loving heavenly Father for His grace, mercy and faithfulness to us, knowing that as long as we were content in whatever our circumstances were, our future was wide open for the Lord to promote and to bless, even as we were fully committed to His service.

And so it was with many of these experiences to look back on, when confronted with a ridiculously long list of needs as we were in Guatemala, that we settled back on the confidence we had in the goodness of the Lord. He promised to provide. He knew all about the things we would need and so we simply brought them to Him in prayer and waited.

The following stories are chosen to highlight what we regularly described as 'God's blatant grace and favour upon this His project'.

As mentioned earlier, the engineers from E.M.I. had provided us with the architectural design and a complete set of detailed drawings. But to further enrich this miracle of provision, we were blessed with the husband and wife team of professional engineers who came and worked on the project full-time. This meant that from the outset, all calculations, estimates and sizing were done to the highest standards. And again we see another miracle of God's perfect timing with our worksite supervisor and his wife coming down from Canada to join the team. Like the engineers, he and his wife wish to remain anonymous but God knows who they are and what great hands-on professional work they did, in service for the Lord whilst they were there in Guatemala.

There were many anonymous financial donors, some who donated their time and many who gave both. One day according to scripture, the Lord Jesus Christ will officiate at an awards giving event, of such magnitude, nothing we have witnessed on earth will compare. (See 1 Cor. 3:11-15). We receive salvation through trusting in what Jesus did for us on Calvary. That's why we say; salvation comes through putting our faith in Christ. We cannot receive salvation by doing good works, like donating our time, talent and treasure, but believers and followers of Christ, will one day receive a reward for the deeds that they have done in the Name of Christ and for His glory. Literally hundreds of volunteers have worked and given towards the creation of the William Cornelius Vocational Training Centre in Guatemala, simply because they believed in the vision and mission statement of such a worthy project. Desiring to please and serve the Lord in participating in the construction of a Christian, technical-high school specifically designed for the young graduates of the various Christian grade schools across Guatemala. These students would typically leave school at grades 6 or perhaps 9. But now they will have an opportunity to find a good job or study at the university.

It is a joy to know that the many young men and women will now have this new opportunity, but the greatest of all thrills what we experience is when we hear of one of these precious young people finding the Lord Jesus Christ as their own, personal Saviour at one of the many spiritual enrichment events enjoyed at the W.C.V.T.C. During those early days of construction, a volunteer team member from our home assembly in Edmonton, Alberta, came over and sat by me at break time. He is typically a straight shooter, not big on small talk, unless he's mocking tea drinkers which I am. He asked me, "Who is going to be handling the electrical installation of this building?" I replied, "At this point in time, I have no idea". His response, "OK, I'll handle the electrical". I sat still for a while as I tried to process what I had just heard. Then I asked, "What does that mean, you'll handle the electrical installation?" I knew he owned an electrical contracting company. He replied, "Don't worry about the electrical

installation I will find the materials, ship them down and organize the installation". I was speechless. I was not aware of the
actual costs involved in this area of construction but I knew we
were looking at several hundred thousand dollars when labour
cost were included. I knew him well enough to know that he was
a man of his word. I looked at him and said "Thank you!" He
simply nodded and went back to what he was doing, prior to our
conversation. From that point on, he conferred with the project
engineer and the worksite supervisor on all aspects of the electrical installation; transformers, cable, wire, pipes and conduits,
panels, switches, breakers, boxes and light fixtures. Like all the
others who had come together to see this work completed, he
was doing what he knew he could do, for the Lord.

A similar situation would happen with all our plumbing
needs as well as all our mechanical needs. Different men who
owned their own businesses in these fields of construction,
simply wrote enquiring what fans and pumps and motors would
be needed? Or, how many wash basins, toilets, and faucets
will the school require? Another follower of Christ asked for
a rough idea as to how many square meters of ceramic wall
tiles we could use; when the container arrived, filled with all
the above materials, there were enough wall tiles to tile the
walls of all six student bathrooms, 6 counter top kitchen areas
as well as all the walls and work benches in our science lab.
The dozen or so boxes that were remaining, were donated to

another of the 'Child Care Plus' grade schools. The icing on the cake of these massive, miraculous provisions from God is that each of the owners of these generous businesses, actually came down to personally install or oversee the installation of these donated gifts.

For those who are students of faith, it's important to be aware that trusting God as our source of supply is not in any way, mind over matter, or trying through mental focus to create your own reality. There's no hocus-pocus here, it's simply knowing that of ourselves we can do nothing. God, who created all things, will do those things which line up with His will and purpose. When Elisha told the widow (2 Kings 4:1-7) to go into your house and shut the door and follow God's instructions given by Elisha, three elements were integral to the miraculous outcome.

1. Getting alone with God. 2. Obeying Him. 3. Expecting a solution to her problem.

From the beginning, God's desire has been to fellowship with His creation. He wants us to enter in and experience His boundless love for us as His children. Getting alone with God then, is paramount to our being able to know Him, to love Him for who He is and not for what He can do for us. It's in those moments of quiet awareness of His presence, when we are most likely to hear His whisper as it resonates in our hearts and minds. Usually a prerequisite to such sacred moments is our willing obedience in following His will and ways. We do this best by spending time in His Word; asking Him to open our under-standing to what we are reading. Asking for wisdom so that we might properly apply what His word is saying to us. Making a commitment to change things in our lives that the Holy Spirit puts His finger on. This might mean a change in our attitude or opinion about something or someone. It might be that what you have just read, convicts you about a habit in your life that you have always felt comfortable about, but now you know that should you continue to practice, it will simply be a sin. The widow collected all the jars she could, then went inside her house and shut the door. This would seem crazy to her neighbours. Her friends wouldn't have encouraged her in this faith venture, so shutting the door on all who would discourage and ridicule was the best thing she could do. She and her sons were now alone with God. All she had to do was trust God and expect Him to come through for her. The element of expectation is the natu-ral-supernatural ingredient in taking a step of faith. We humans are still earthbound and so we still function with our human nature. But as believers in the Lord, we are humans who are 'in Christ' (2 Cor. 5 & 6). We have been reconciled to God through the death of God's Son, Who died for us, so that we might have life eternal. Now when God The Father looks at me, He sees me in His Son Jesus. He sees the righteousness of Christ in me! Not through anything I have done but because I have put my faith in the cleansing power of the shed blood of Christ. So as a man or a woman who is 'in Christ', we have the Holy Spirit living within our being. It is He, who inspires this supernatural element of expectation we exhibit as we put our faith in God. What did the widow woman do to show this act of expectant faith? She picked up the jar that had oil in it and started to pour it out into the empty jars! "Quick!" she says to her sons. "Get me another empty jar!" and another and another until there was more than enough to solve her problem.

Now it bears saying that God doesn't always do what we ask of Him regardless of the spiritual gymnastics that we go through. I once prayed for a man who had suffered all his life with an extreme speech impediment. We were together on the evening shift. I asked him if he believed God could heal him, he said yes. I asked if he would allow me to anoint him with oil and lay hands on him and pray for him in the Name of Jesus. He said yes. I did so. I felt full of faith. I suggested he go believing that he was healed. The next day when he came into the workshop, he avoided me. He continued to avoid me from that time on. I felt very embarrassed and conflicted. It's something I have never forgotten, but it didn't stop me trusting in the Lord to answer prayer. It did make me wiser in my under-standing that God will have His way in someone's life, not my way. He is God, not some kind of Genie that grants our wishes because we stroke Him the right way.

The school was designed to have aluminum framed glass doors and windows. So for the sake of security, we began, as funds permitted, to get the windows installed all-round the ground floor. And before getting the rather expensive glass double doors installed, we decided to install the more secure, steel roll doors. We had enough money to install three but we needed seven. Our prayer continued that we would be able financially, to purchase the various building materials as we needed them.

We had kept in touch down the years with missionary friends from our South Africa days, who were now retired in British Columbia, Canada. The husband in his 90's had recently gone home to be with the Lord. His wife had written to tell us that they had been planning to send a contribution toward the building project; she hoped we could use the money for where it was most needed. Here again the Lord knew that we were praying specifically for $3000.00 in order to pay for the installation of the remaining four roll doors. Her cheque, to our amazement was the exact amount we had been praying for. God is good all the time, but not just for certain people, He is good to all who seek Him and call upon Him. As I was going through the local Yellow Pages, looking for a company who could give me a final quote on the roll doors, I was almost down to the end of the list, before getting a positive response.

The gentleman sounded quite excited on the phone and agreed to come over within the hour. Luis arrived on time and presented himself in a very businesslike way; he explained the quality of the product and the manner in which he and his sons would install the strong, secure roll doors. He spent ample time measuring the various openings in the building, where we needed the doors. As we returned to the office to discuss the price, tears suddenly appeared in his eyes and he started to cry. We wondered what was going on with this man that he was unable to hold in his emotions. He controlled himself and told us his story. In the early hours of the morning he had been desperately crying out to God, saying that if He didn't send him some work immediately, he would have to close his business. My phone call came at 9:00 am. We were all praising the Lord and joining him in his open show of emotion. Pauline was in the process of writing a cheque for the deposit for the door, when again, what he told us next brought on a new wave of praise and thanksgiving . He said, "Because this is the work of the Lord and that it is an answer to prayer, the first roll door I install will be a tithe unto Him". Pauline and Debbie one of the work team members from Alberta, started to cry; we all rejoiced together, holding hands as we prayed a special blessing upon Luis and his family and his business It wasn't unusual to see groups of guests or volunteers or at times with our local workers, praying God's blessings upon each other and upon the work we were all involved in together.

Teams of volunteers were coming now on average of one per month. Repeat teams were especially a joy to receive, as they knew what to expect and always made sure the building trades were well represented. Jobs and materials were assembled ahead of time so that on arrival, the work was attacked with gusto and progress was impressive. Every team had ample non-skilled labourers to help fetch and carry. Each team had a team leader who worked closely with our engineer and worksite supervisor. It was exciting to see our new friends and old, from churches across Canada installing electrical pipes and fittings, drain pipes, mixing and pouring concrete, cutting and building wash basin tops and 6 kitchen workstations, 6 dental hygiene units and cupboards as well as a full 20' X 10' kitchen of lower and upper cupboards, all built and prepared in Edmonton, then shipped down, assembled and installed on site before our eyes. We had team members welding steel beams for the roof covering and laying cinder blocks wall after wall. Canadian dry-walling skills were greatly appreciated in converting the large administration room into the required offices, bathrooms and reception area. The Lord just kept sending the right people at the right time, along with just the right amount of money to keep the project moving forward.

Along with volunteer work teams, we tried to keep a full time team of national workers also. These hard working men were amazingly skillful in all areas of construction. They kept going almost non-stop with the block laying, concrete column pouring and plastering of the walls and workshop ceilings.

It was always a special highlight to get together with our national workers at the farewell B.B.Q. for the Canadian teams. It was hilarious to watch as these 5'- 6" Mayans would give the 6' Canadians a run for their money with the 'tug o' war' contests. Another Guatemalan tradition thoroughly enjoyed by the Canadians was the lighting of the fireworks. Where normally quiet, serious business men would get carried away like a bunch of deprived children. Doling out large amounts of money in order to enjoy firecrackers going off, double the size of litre pop bottles, with explosions loud enough to cause a tectonic shift a mile below the school's foundations! Well not that loud but it did sound like a war zone.

Surviving the fireworks and the fun, the building was beginning to look like a school. Another priceless gift that the work teams brought with them, was contagious joy and encouragement. Each day beginning with devotional sharing and prayer, with excellent fellowship mixed in with the sounds of shovels and hammers and saws. God is always present to watch over His work. We felt Him strongly when the teams were with us, but knew He was still right there, even after they left.

CHAPTER 8

FAITH AND FINISHING PHASE

How often do we hear it repeated, 'It's not how you start that counts, it's how you finish'. This maxim is true in every area of life, whether we're talking about running a race, developing a career, building a school or serving the Lord. We all make mistakes as we go through the early stages of whatever it is we are learning at the time. The idea is that we don't keep repeating them as we progress through life. But the greatest tragedy facing our world today is the thought that we can become good enough by our own efforts to please God in order to have entrance into heaven when we die. I say this for the millions alive today, who believe that because they are good people, who have helped the needy and have hurt no-one, that God will welcome them into His Kingdom. This is a tragedy, because those who place themselves in this category are actually thumbing their nose at God by saying, "I didn't need You to send Your Son Jesus to die for me, I'm good enough in my own strength and righteousness". And they are going stubbornly through life under that assumption hoping they are right, even though, as I have quoted John 3:16 before, that because God loves the people of the world so much, He sent His Son to take the punishment for our sin, so that those who believe He did this for them, actually for them as a person, will not perish, (miss heaven) but have everlasting life. This is the ultimate in finishing well.

When Pauline and I returned to Canada we spent the next five years working as pastors in a large senior's residence in Edmonton, Alberta. What a rich and marvelous experience that was, visiting and ministering to these older adults, many of whom were old enough to be our parents even though we were in our late sixties. I'm going to be talking about our work at the Shepherd's Care Foundation later in this book, but one thing I want to mention here is that it is possible to recognize a life that is finishing well. By 2006, we were reaching the finishing phase at the William Cornelius Vocational Training Centre. Thanks to the Lord's faithfulness in prompting several people to send some large donations, we were able to put the roofing on, get the marble tile flooring installed throughout the building and install many of the doors and windows. But we felt particularly blessed by the many small donations that were given. We would prioritize these gifts with any item that was urgent at the time. Usually this was building materials or tools, or we would save it in order to accumulate enough to buy steel for the many railings and window bars.

We certainly give thanks and want to express our deep gratitude to each and every person who sacrificed in order to help in the building of this incredible school. In sacrificing we are investing in the Kingdom of God. We acknowledge every gift with thankfulness before the Lord, for He is the giver of all good gifts. Like spiritual gifs, some of the donations at the school are more up-front and obvious than others, yet we know that all our deeds of kindness will be rewarded if done in the Name of the Lord.

One very up-front donation was from a couple with unique skills in the area of landscaping. They asked if they could plan and install the central patio feature as well as take on the development and planting of all the trees and flower beds. We knew their hearts were right and that what they wanted to do was please and serve the Lord. So with joy we said yes. With their team's return from southern Alberta, we saw the transformation of the garden areas both inside and out. Beautiful flowers and trees all-round the building and a gorgeous waterfall at the far end of the central patio, displaying peaceful calm water falling and cascading over terraced rocks into a pool surrounded by a rock garden with a backdrop of tropical plants and flowers. The ambience is sweet and tranquil. A place to worship and study.

Our plan was to open the school in the January of 2007. Much was still needed to be done of course, but our thinking was to finish what we could before the grand opening and continue after this historic event until the last item on the job list was completed. Little did we know what tests still lay up ahead.

Thanks to a previous team member who had his own painting business, we were able to get the whole building painted inside and out. We hired a professional local company to do the outside, using spray painting equipment. All inside walls were painted by volunteer team members, when we were between teams, the painting never stopped. Pauline took it upon herself to keep painting the classrooms and laboratory walls until they were all finished, totaling sixteen rooms.

Two huge water tanks had been installed underground, early in the construction process and water was trucked in every three or four days in order to have enough water always at the ready for construction purposes. Now that the building was almost finished, the water was needed to supply the many toilets, wash basins and kitchen areas. Pumps were donated and brought down from Canada. Pipes were installed and before we knew it, we went from having to use one inside toilet and one 'outside' toilet, to having about thirty toilets to choose from! It was time now, to eliminate our one outside toilet. It was affectionately called, 'The Royal Alex'. It was a simple, humble structure, made with planks of rough wood with a galvanized roof. It was as rudimentary a facility as one could find any-where in the world, yet it brought 'relief' to hundreds, just when they needed it. It got its auspicious name from a senior vol-unteer who built it, Alex from Ontario. The name 'Royal' was added to help capture it's description as a throne room, but trust me, after several years of use, no amount of gilded trim-mings could help a visitor want to linger in order to admire its surroundings! Nevertheless, welcome it was, to the many who paid a visit. Not many tears were shed however, when water was finally pumped up to the battery of water tanks on the roof, giving functionality to all the flushable units inside. It came time to quite unceremoniously dismantle the Royal Alex and fill in the earthen receptacle over which much thought and respite had taken place. Momentum was gathering now as we worked our way through 2006. Following the team from Crowsnest Pass in January, we were blessed with the ongoing work of the landscapers, even into February. March brought a spurt of exciting progress with a returning team from Kelowna. It was whilst they were with us that the last remaining retaining wall was built, bringing security and stability to the school now on all sides of this great project. Final drains and plumbing were going in, along with Canadian expertise in dry walling. It goes without saying of course, that while all this construction work was happening, much preparation was under way in order for us to be ready to begin operating a technical school in a matter of ten months.

As with the need to have a qualified engineer in order to build a school building, we now needed a qualified director to give leadership to the academic side of running a school. Edna was already on board as the overall administrator–now we were asking the Lord as to who we could hire to fill this auspicious and historical position. Anna Marie was the one who came to be the first Director of the W.C.V.T.C. She set to work on putting together what the Guatemalan Ministry of Education calls, the 'Proyecto Educativo'. This is basically a portfolio of every document relating to the makeup of the school's vision, mission statement, budget, facility, adminis-tration, staff, teachers, students and subjects. It includes the full year's calendar of classes and events. And they wanted this ahead of time! When I asked how this was possible, in that we still didn't know so many of the details, I was told that it was normal in these circumstances to fill in the unknowns with 'phantom' details. It was good to know that Anna Marie knew how to assemble this huge amount of material. She also assisted us in helping to interview prospective staff members. So much prayer was going into this preparation phase, mainly because we knew that once staff has been hired and students registered, there can be no more delays or postponements. Once a school is open, it goes on indefinitely. More on this later.

No sooner had the Kelowna team left, another returning team from Newfoundland came. The Lord was so kind in sending to us these wonderful teams of men and women. We never stipulated who could or couldn't come, (other than the minimum age of eighteen) whoever came, young or old, fit or unfit, skilled or unskilled; we were always able to suit a task to everyone.

Everyone worked really hard. It was always a joy to receive them, to serve them and to bless them. While the Nufie team was with us, lots of finishing jobs were done. Block work on the third floor, welding in the multi-purpose hall, tile work and painting. A couple of dozen white boards were installed and the first fifty student desks, donated from a college in the U.S.A. were repaired and placed in what would be the first two classrooms that would be used in the school.

We received an e-mail from the P.A.O.C. desk of E.R.D.O. asking if we could use some really elegant tables. One of the things we had been praying about was furniture. We had none, other than the student desks. Our reply of course was, "Yes, we could use some tables". Later in the year we received a container from the E.R.D.O. warehouse with seventy five, absolutely beautiful, four foot by two foot polished rose wood tables and a couple of dozen small round table also. All still in their wrapping paper from the factory. They had brass fittings and feet. Ideal for school desks in many of our classrooms and just in time! Once again, confirmation of God's promise to us, 'He will provide all that you need to complete the work'.

During our previous itinerary across Canada we were visiting our P.A.O.C. churches, mainly to report what God was doing in people's lives through the building of this much needed school, but we also took the opportunity of inviting people to consider sponsoring a student at the soon to be opened – William Cornelius Vocational Training Centre. For those who did, they would now have that unique and special satisfaction of knowing that a life was being changed for the better; providing wonderful opportunities for open doors with job potential, but also of being directly responsible for bringing this real young person into an amazing Christian environment, where lives would be enriched with the truths of God's Word while, at the same time, receiving all the usual high school subjects for grades 10,11 and 12, along with the added benefit of being trained in a new profession.

The first profession we were planning to launch at the start of the new year was Computer Technology. Qualified teachers for all required subjects were now being sought who would themselves produce the already approved curriculum through the Guatemalan Ministry of Education. Three years later, the successful graduates would receive a High School diploma and an officially recognized certificate of competency for their particular professional training. These diplomas and certificates would now give options to these capable young people of becoming gainfully employed or, should they wish to continue their education, they would be able to enroll at the University of Guatemala where costs of registration and course material are kept at a minimum.

Another wonderful thing happened while we were home on furlough. Following the Sunday evening service at the church in Goderich, Ontario, we were invited to a home for refreshments and fellowship. Here I was introduced to one of the church members who was also a member of the local chapter of the Rotary Club. He asked if there was some particular project within the overall project that they could consider as a joint venture in concert with the Guatemala City chapter. I explained that as of yet, we hadn't even begun focusing on the needs of the school library furnishings that would be needed along with several quotes. He assured me that he would bring it to his committee and contact his Guatemalan counterpart. Again we gave our thanks to the Lord and express our gratitude to the Goderich (no pun intended I assure you) chapter of the Rotary Club. Because of this very timely donation from these two groups of volunteers, we were able to purchase a photocopying machine, a computer, eight library book stands, two dozen chairs as well as all the required text books for the first year of operation. Once again without any stress or strain, everything we needed was being provided according to His promise.

Our friend John Linquist, one of the E.M.I. engineers was now living in Guatemala in the San Cristobal area with his wife Sharon. The E.M.I. ministry was growing to the point now, where it became necessary for them to open a regional office, serving all of Central America. John & Sharon were as excited and enthusiastic about the development of the W.C.V.T.C. as we were and made it their business to make regular visits, always looking for ways to help out in any way they could.

Consequently there would be times when we would have four or five volunteer engineers actually working on some mathematical calculation in the design work, at one time. One of the many blessings that came out of having the E.M.I. team on board was the creative way in which these engineers began to invest their time, talent and treasure into the lives of student engineers from Guatemala. Not only did they help in training them 'on the job' but in some cases they even sponsored them through their schooling.

One day John asked me if I had a plan for the installation of the telephone network for the school. I didn't. All the conduits were in, but that was all. He went on to say he had a friend who would be willing to come down and install a complete system at no cost to the school. This would include a switchboard and about twenty extension phones. Once again, I was thanking the Lord, thanking John and before long I was thanking David for his gracious spirit and generosity in actually

174

coming to Guatemala and installing our telephone system. David is not his full name of course. He, like so many others who have worked tirelessly and given so generously to this school project, are not looking for personal recognition at all. They are committed in service to the Lord and have done what they have done for His glory, not for their own glory. For this reason some who have given extensively, have indicated that they wish to remain anonymous.

The classrooms and laboratories were designed to accommodate thirty students. The word was out that our initial specialty was going to be Computer Technology. We were praying that the Lord would show us what to do about equipping the presently empty computer lab with computers and workstations. It was about six months before the grand opening when Pastor Randy Tonn sent an e-mail asking us if we could use 60 computers complete with workstations? He explained that a company in Edmonton was bound by contract to replace their computers and equipment every two years and rather than throw them out they wanted to send them somewhere they could be put to good use.

Excitement at how the Lord keeps His promises never gets old. We expressed our willingness to Pastor Randy that yes, we would love to help this company by taking these perfectly good computer off their hands. The computers were properly packed along with all the dismantled workstations and placed in the huge container that was also bringing electrical, plumbing, cupboard, mechanical, wall tile and pumping equipment and materials. The container arrived three weeks before the volunteer work team. This team consisted of nine electricians, each with a helper, a plumbing crew, installing the toilets, carpenters, painters, graphic artists, dry wall workers, tilers, as well as a crew of hardware and software technicians, who worked extra-long hours in order to finish the installation of the computer laboratory.

The carpenter crew did much to begin the building and installing of what would become the Dental Hygiene laboratory. Sink units were installed in six different places around the school as were all the lights, switches, outlets and electrical panels. One of the last items to be installed by this uniquely assembled team was the drop ceiling tile 'T' bar which was installed throughout the building. People had come together to work on this team at their own expense, from British Columbia, Alberta, Manitoba and Ontario. And what an amazing difference we could now see. Time was moving on and we were all putting our best foot forward in order to be ready for the grand opening on the 13th and 14th January 2007.

Painting was basically finished. The electrical connections were complete except for the third floor. Office furniture was purchased thanks to the consistent flow of designated project funds coming through our World Missions Department, E.R.D.O. in Ontario, Canada.

A beautiful wall plaque was installed at the foyer of the main entrance to the school. We called it our 'Wall of Honour' as we listed all the names of work teams, and long term volunteers, acknowledging our thanks to each of them. Amongst all the Canadian teams, we had three teams also who came from the U.S.A. From the outset of the enormous building project until the opening day, there were over 65 teams who came. They were from the provinces of: British Columbia, Alberta, Manitoba, Ontario & Newfoundland as well as Florida and Colorado. Many churches sent multiple teams multiple times. We honour each and every individual who is represented on the plaque. There is a saying in Spanish: 'Dios le recompensa' which means: 'God will repay you'. We know this was never your motive for doing what you did in coming to serve, but it's true nevertheless. God is no man's debtor and His blessings will follow your obedience.

Interviews for potential future staff was going well. Contracts were being prepared. The internet and phone service was now working. Much planning was now complete. School uniforms had been decided on. The computer lab was set up and ready to go. Dental Hygiene chairs had been specially made to go with the dental quad units that were in place. Dental lamps had been mounted from the ceiling and wow! This place looked incredible!

The Edmonton and Crowsnest Pass teams that came at the end of 2006 along with our daughter Tracy and landscapers, Ernie, Debbie & Brandy worked incredibly hard to help us get ready. Laboratories were readied, classrooms were waiting now for students, and the library was now set up. A bank of computers were also installed and functioning in the library.

Thanks to different team members, we even had a good variety of musical instruments for our music room. Special wall tiles had been made and installed into the cement walls displaying the respective bathrooms for the ladies and the gents.

The school's ten 'Values' were also embedded into the walls at different random places, so that the eye could catch them unexpectedly. These values are: Love, Respect, Faithfulness, Loyalty, Honesty, Passion, Righteousness, Loving Kindness, Willingness, and Example. All these of course were prepared in the Spanish language.

One of the senior volunteers painted a great big welcome sign over the reception area. Another young artist painted a mural of a grape vine, incorporating the Cross, showing the Vine, the branches and unbelievably real looking bunches of grapes. All emphasizing the school's theme taken from John 15:5 where Jesus says "I am the vine, you are the branches. He who abides in Me, and I in him, bears much fruit; for without Me you can do nothing". This can still be seen on the Board Room wall.

The place was looking marvellous. Yet, we were now reeling from some news we had just received. The bank which we used for the school's account, one of the biggest in the country, had just declared bankruptcy, rendering us penniless as we headed for the school's opening in just a matter of weeks.

Chapter 9

'WALKING BY FAITH

The day before the bank crashed, we had just deposited a special donation into the school account of $30,000. This was given by a friend of the school project as a financial cushion, to help cover all the extra expenses that would incur for the start up in January 2007; we also had $4,000 in the account. The day after we deposited our startup funds, we were informed that all accounts were frozen and that over time, as the bank's assets were liquidated, we would eventually receive about .40 on the dollar. And that all dollar accounts would have to wait until all the local Quetzal accounts had been dealt with first. Ours was a dollar account.

Prayer is the God given supernatural communication facility that is available to everyone. Faith is also a divine gift but is given only to those who believe in the giver. God is the giver and He grants large measures of faith to all who will trust in

His Son as the only one who has ever been able to live a perfect life, acceptable to His heavenly Father. Jesus then willingly died on the Cross of Calvary to appease God's righteous judgement upon a world of sin, so that, as we repent of our sin and thank Jesus for taking our sin upon Himself, acknowledging that He did it for us, we then become a follower of Christ. Freed from sin and the power of sin. Declared righteous in the sight of God, justified through faith in Christ Jesus. Which means that we sinful creatures, can walk with God now – freed from sin – as though we had never sinned. It was this powerful gift from God that we were now leaning upon, quite heavily. Everything was arranged for the opening of the W.C.V.T.C. in just a few weeks, yet all our tangible resources had just gone poof!

Let me share a short list of commitments we were bound to fulfil; teachers had been hired and administration staff and maintenance staff were all expecting to begin work in the January 2007. Students were coming to school to register, which in itself was historic. About 30 people had booked flights, from Canada and the U.S.A. in order to attend the opening. The paperwork registering the school with the Ministry of Education was all finally in order after the marathon of running the bureaucratic gauntlet for so many years.

We began to pray and fast. After the third day the Lord spoke to us and said, "Everything is in order, go ahead and open". What an incredible relief for us. Our daily devotions only strengthened our faith and resolve to reiterate that this was the Lord's work. His project. His school, hearing from Him we felt at peace in our spirits that the Lord would have us open the school on schedule.

People were asking what they should do. Were we going to cancel the opening? We replied telling them to stay with the plan, that we would hold our opening celebrations as planned on the 13th and 14th January with the first day of school being the 15th.

We knew the Lord wasn't surprised by the bank going 'belly up' so we trusted that He had a plan B. which would actually be His plan A. There was a strangely exciting sense of adventure that I had never experienced before. In a country where you can be jailed for writing unsupported cheques, we knew that our hearts were right before the Lord, so either we were testing Him or He was testing us, or both. The test was on and there would be no turning back. We did remind the Lord that He had promised to provide all that we would need. We did not believe that He would let us down. To paraphrase Psalm 138: 7 -8. 'When I find myself walking into unexpected trouble, Your hand oh Lord will fully protect me so that I can complete the work You sent me to do'.

God provided us with His holy Word for guidance and for instruction. Another major function of the Word is that in times of trouble we can receive encouragement from it and assurance. But it's really only when we use faith in its application in our life circumstances, that the power of the Word gets a chance to truly manifest itself. Faith, after all, is the evidence of things not seen. Can you imagine the depth of gratitude we felt that December, as we received word that the church which had sent several work teams down, from Newfoundland, felt that as they had not sent a team for a while, wanted to donate a cheque. The cheque in question was for $10,000.

God is faithful to His word and to His children. And it is because His children in the churches are sensitive to His voice which is constantly speaking to them, that so much is actually taking place on what we call 'the mission field'. Not only in Guatemala but in all the countries of the world. It's only as we are able to give sacrificially that God's Word goes forth whether at home or abroad.

What a marvelous and majestic grand opening we were able to have. The whole of the two days celebrations was about giving thanks and glory to the Lord. We had guests and dignitaries from near and far, including our General Superintendent of the P.A.O.C. but, our praise and worship was of course, only to our wonderful Lord and Saviour.

It was truly a joyous time. The building was not quite finished but it looked beautiful. Many friends from Canada and the U.S.A. enjoyed mingling with many Guatemalan guests. The music and the testimonials were exceptional, giving God the glory for all He has done. Try and catch the atmosphere with all this excitement. Thrilling everyone's hearts to realize that we were surrounded by the unquestionable evidence of a multifaceted miracle. God is still a miracle working God! He is still dispatching His mighty angels to protect and guard His children. It's because we know this to be true, that we can better accept the apparent bad things that happen in our lives. A tragic death in the family. A painful illness. A terrible car accident. Do we throw our hands up in despair, questioning God every time things don't go the way we think they should? Or are we able to see through the hurt surrounding us and make out the outline of our Father's hand? God will never cause evil to come our way but there will be occasions when for whatever reason, only He knows, He will allow the enemy's tornado to get through. An inexplicable head on collision claiming a whole family. A two year old infant drowned in a neighbour's pool. Why shouldn't we get angry at God? As I said earlier, I don't have all the answers, but I do know we would do well to be careful how we react before our Creator. God is God and is always working for our highest good. We should try to think of these terrible tragedies from the point of view of eternity. Where any 'innocent', taken from us, is immediately rejoicing in the young choirs of heaven, surrounded by constant new discoveries of all that God's special dwelling place has to offer. This surely can be the only good thing that we can say about the scourge of abortion. Every life that is snuffed out at the hands of doctors and charlatans alike, according to God's word, that precious, eternal soul when forced to be absent from the body, is present with the Lord (2 Corinthians 5: 1-11).

Life is more than precious, it is sacred, because it belongs to God. God is the eternal arbiter on life and death. Governments, councils and so-called authority groups who have taken it upon themselves to even think that they are qualified to make decisions relating to life and death, are attempting to grab the reins of control out of God's hands in order to steer human morality towards a more liberal, progressive position. It might look as though it's working in the short term, but as history constantly tries to teach us, the strutting pride of the human heart will eventually trip over its own boasting feet.

God loves us, yes. He is compassionately gracious, yes. But remember this; He will not be mocked. Though, it is never too late to seek God's forgiveness for our disobedience.

Elephants don't like being mocked. During our stay in the Eastern Transvaal of South Africa, we would hear stories of people trying to enjoy a visit to the Kruger National Park but in doing so, were running the risk of being chased off by an elephant.

It was later discovered that drivers for the food delivery companies, taking supplies to the various camps, were stopping near to the elephants and throwing stones at them. I remember seeing a picture in the local newspaper of a large delivery van, showing two 5" holes in the side of the van about 4' apart. The article was warning people not to tantalize the elephants. The following picture showed a completely flattened Volkswagen Beetle. It appeared that the people in the Beetle had stopped to admire the elephants shorty after being teased. They escaped with their lives just before their car was trampled.

Just prior to our leaving South Africa for Australia, we decided to take a final trip into the Kruger National Park, which was close to our home, to go and see the animals in the wild. We did see many magnificent animals, including giraffe, springbok, baboons and sable, we almost killed a cheetah that was bounding along in the long grass, who jumped straight in front of our vehicle, a V.W. Beetle. V.W.Beetles were very popular in South Africa. The cheetah stopped, I stopped and there we were, staring at each other. Maybe it was hungry and wondering if it could eat this strange, round thing making a buzzing noise. We don't know, but after admiring the beautiful creature for about five seconds it continued on its way. We really sympathize with the tourists who were almost killed by the elephant because we had a very similar experience.

Driving through the game reserve, you see whatever you can from the dirt road. You are told to stay in your car at all times for obvious reasons. Occasionally you will come upon a 'loop road'. These make it possible to get closer to the river banks where you can often see the hippopotamus and crocodiles. We saw one of these loop roads coming up ahead with several cars already lined up along the top of the river bank. We joined the line of cars which were moving slowly around the loop. Other cars dropped in behind us, so we were hemmed in back and front. Everyone there had their cameras out, straining their necks to see what it was that was moving the thick bushes and trees. Pauline was at the wheel which in South African cars is on the right, the same as Britain.

I was leaning out of the window with the camera. Simon now four and Tracy three years of age were in the back of the car. I was just saying to Pauline and my father. "Well, I think there's something coming up the river bank..." When, there it was! This huge, bull elephant's head coming out from thick foliage of the trees. First I saw its big baggy ears flapping, trunk sticking straight out only ten feet away from us. I said "Polly, go back!" She wasn't taking orders and there was nowhere to go as several cars had us blocked in. Pauline was however, able to give orders. Her tone made it quite clear that this was not open to negotiation. She said, "You drive!" Now under normal circumstances, what happened in the next four seconds would not be possible but we were both a lot younger then. In one smooth move we switched seats. By this time, the cars in front had seen what was happening and had started to get out of the way. I was able now to move fast enough to stay in front of the elephant. This encounter with danger was a little too close for my liking and I had a word with the Lord about it later, suggesting that my guardian angels not sleep on the job.

We have found ourselves in dangerous circumstances many times along our journey, but not so present and clear as one morning in the August of 2009, Guatemala City. We were preparing the upcoming, first ever graduation ceremony at the William Cornelius school. Much still needed to be done though, before this auspicious event could take place. We now had students from the classes of 2007, 2008 and 2009. So with the close of the Guatemalan school year being October, it was necessary to hold the exams, farewell celebrations and graduation ceremonies before the middle of October. With many of our students being sponsored from churches and individuals across Canada, it was also important to give our whole student body an early Christmas party. Teachers and students together would enjoy some traditional Christmas food and music as well as each student receiving a gift. Sponsored students would also be given whatever special gift that was sent down from their sponsors. In order to be able to give the sponsored students the correct amount of money, I needed to go to the bank, in advance, to get lots of correct change. This particular day, Pauline and I came out of the bank with a large brown bag of small change. We were obviously spotted by a rough looking guy sat at the gate of the bank. He was already on his cell phone before we started the car. Being alert in

Guatemala is par for the course; so as we were driving to the school, my antennas were up. Usually the congestion on the Calzada Roosevelt is more of a nuisance than a help but this day it proved to be a wonderful help. Traffic was heavy but moving along quite nicely. All four lanes were full which prevented the usual stream of motor bikes from winding in and out from one lane to another. Most bike riders are couriers and delivery men who ride low powered, noisy two strokes. They dress for the weather and always have a shoulder bag to carry their documents in. So, when I saw the speed bike with two riders wearing fancy leathers and flashy helmets trying to gain ground from three cars back, I began to ask the Lord to keep us safe. I said nothing to Pauline.

There had been a spurt of brutal robberies by men on motor bikes over the past six months and it was in the news that a bill was in its final stages to make it a criminal offence to have more than one person on a motor bike. Sure enough, the bike with the red stripe was getting closer. I had a right turn coming up, so I made the turn quickly without signaling. He almost didn't make it round the tight turn. He corrected and tried to pass me but there wasn't room as I steered to prevent his progress. Amazingly the road was clear at the next intersection. I made the left turn more aggressively than I would normally and accelerated away; now going downhill slightly, the bike was certain to be able to pass and cut me off, but as he made his move I turned right. We were now three blocks away from the school where we have an armed guard 24/7. The bike rider corrected again and almost passed me but just braked in time to keep from running into a parked car. He then made a quick 'U' turn as he caught sight of the sub-police station a block away from the school. I saw in my rear view mirror that he whipped round the corner to go around the block and cut me off but that block winds round an extra block distance, giving me a chance to make it to the school gate a couple of seconds before he did.

I sounded my horn to alert the guard to open the automatic gate. It was now opening as the rider of the bike was obviously yelling instructions at the top of his voice, but with his helmet covering his face and my window being closed. I could only guess that he was asking me to turn over the money. The fact that I was looking down the barrel of his six shooter was another clue. The gate which opens to the left, running on a steel rail, had never moved so slowly as on this occasion. It was as if time had slowed down. I saw the gun waving at me, I saw his head frantically moving, I saw his pillion rider, gesticulating, and I heard Pauline quite calmly saying, "What does he want?" completely unaware of what was taking place. When I knew that the gate was sufficiently open, I hit the gas pedal and shot forward. The guard asked the robber what he wanted, he already had put the gun away and replied that he was asking for directions, then drove away. Unfortunately it was not the end of the story.

As already mentioned, many gang related robberies had been happening and it seemed apparent that this was their way of financing their operation. As we made our way home the following day, the traffic one block over from the school was moving very slowly. The police were moving everyone over to the inside lane, in order to pass a stationery vehicle at the intersection. We were horrified to see that the two occupants, a man and woman, had been shot several times. But it was only the following day in conversation with the company adjacent to the school that we learned, the people who had been shot had been doing business with them and were driving a vehicle almost identical to ours. We don't know for sure of course, but it would appear that the robbers were intent on getting even and had shot the wrong people, only God knows. For many in Guatemala, life has become very cheap. Gang members are not only robbing those who earn a living through going to work every day, they also entrap other young people in order to force them to become new members of their gang. This often means the killing of an innocent person who is just walking along the street at the time of initiation. Bus drivers and taxi drivers are killed if they won't pay a 'toll' for using a street controlled by the gang. Kidnapping for ransom is common and rarely ends well as the person is often passed along from one gang to the next. Young people, especially those who are born into a poor part of the town or village, have very little hope of ever being able to do well for themselves or their potential family. Not everyone gets to go to school. Those who do, usually only go to grade six. Much is being done though through sponsored schooling in order to give these precious young people a chance to dream.

Chapter 10

NEW BEGINNINGS

1 5th January 2007. The grand opening was now a memory, albeit very fresh. Most of the guests were out sightseeing or making their way back home. We at the school were saying 'Hello' to our first class of students. Twenty four new expectant faces. Twelve boys and twelve girls, all between the ages of 16 and 20, depending on how old they were when they started school in grade one. They had been the seniors in their previous school, now they were starting again with wonder and perhaps a little trepidation. Knowing how historic this occasion was, we wanted to meet this first group of precious Guatemalan young people who would experience this great, God given idea for the next three years. This particular group of excited students would receive grades 10, 11 and 12 high school education as well as getting a specialty in Computer Technology. Some were from rural towns a bus ride away but most were

from the poor, outlying areas of Guatemala City and the city of Mixco. All had completed grade 9, but would require remedial help to bring up their level of math and language skills due to the poor standard of education among the teaching staff in the surrounding grade schools. We got them to form a semi-circle and I sat in the middle facing them. I introduced Pauline and myself and gave a brief explanation about the vision of the W.C.V.T.C.

We asked them to share their name and where they were from; I noticed they were all quite shy, yet full of anticipation of what was happening in their lives. About half of them had come up through the Child Care Plus sponsorship programme. I was able to assure them that all of them at this early stage in the life of the school, would be sponsored throughout their time here.

At the time of writing, the school is in its tenth year of operation and is growing each year. There are always many more students than available sponsorships. Should you wish to become a sponsor, becoming an integral part of a person's life, you will be providing in a truly tangible way, a treasured opportunity to receive excellent education and job training in a marvelous Christian environment. Changing the direction of a life for both time and potentially for eternity. If you believe that God is prompting you to play such a part in a young person's life, you can find more information by calling P.A.O.C. 1-905-542-7400 asking to be put through to the E.R.DO. Department.

Or by going to the following website: www.erdo.ca after which you can open News & Resources.

As I reflect on the direction my life has taken, I can see the hand of God in bringing about a change in my own childhood dream of becoming a carpenter.

At the secondary modern school that I attended as a teenager, I was really good at woodwork and reasonably good at metalwork. My older brother Eric excelled at artwork and became an artist in a variety of areas. My oldest brother John was a joiner-carpenter. My very good friend Jesus had been a carpenter, so now, I wanted to be a carpenter. But one cold, wet day, I came home from school complaining of pain in my knees. My knees were becoming stiff and extremely painful. The doctor diagnosed my problem – it was infantile rheumatoid arthritis. After several days of watching my knees swelling up, I was unable to walk. The pain was excruciating. I was off school for three months and confined to bed rest and pain killers. The swelling eventually went down and I returned to school. I have never had a reoccurrence of this problem since.

However on leaving school and looking to find a job as a carpenter, well, I do remember having a serious attack of disappointment. The youth employment office in our local town, had agents who were there to offer advice to parents and youths, who were due to be leaving school. I went along with my father and when the agent asked me what kind of work I would like to do, I quite firmly said, "Carpentry, I want to be a carpenter!" He looked at me, then at my file folder in his hand and said, "You can't be a carpenter! That kind of job will kill you. It's outside work. Out in the cold and wet weather. Up ladders and on building sites. You need a job that is inside. I'll send you to Joseph Adamson's to be an apprentice machinist". And that was that. There was no further discussion. He had in his hand my medical report, detailing my indisputable medical condition with the list and dates of my visits to the doctor's office, X Rays plus lab tests. So, having no idea what a machinist did, I couldn't possibly know what a momentous 'shift' this would prove to be in the direction of life for this fifteen year old.

I received an excellent, practical preparation for life in the workforce. I was a machinist technician for the next twenty seven years before going into the ministry full time. I have never been out of a job because every place we have lived, there has been a demand for machinists. The painful bout with rheumatoid arthritis made the difference in the direction of my life; only later was I able to see the faint, but sure, outline of the hand of God.

The students spoke quietly as we tried to encourage them to relax. This was after all, their first meeting as a group together. I wasn't their teacher but they couldn't know this at the time. I explained that this was a school that God had put in place and that He had His hand on their lives with wonderful plans to bless them and use them for His glory. Of course, it's true that you don't have to attend a Christian school in order to experience the blessing of God on your life but for these young people to be coming from the rough environments of the areas surrounding Guatemala City, it would certainly appear to be a place of peace and safety.

Once they got into the routine of their classes, getting them to go home in the afternoon became something of an issue. They loved being within the confines of the W.C.V.T.C. even with its rules and strict discipline. We loved them and cared for them as we did our own children. There was always lots of laughter and sounds of joy. The key word that we sought to emphasize at all times with regard to all levels of interaction was, 'respect'. Guatemala, like most countries of our world has an unspoken cast system. Wealthy, upper class, mestizos, who are the middle class, and Mayans, who are treated as the lower class. It is generally accepted that all classes have some mixed blood in their family lines and all strata of society have further social divisions within their identified level of society. The W.C.V.T.C. is designed to be available to all levels but is particularly open to provide sponsored opportunities to those young men and women who historically fail to receive a higher education only because the finances are not there.

Many of our graduates have gone on to truly excel in the field of study they found open to them on leaving school. Some have taken advantage of scholarships offered to them from Universities in the United States and in Japan. One young man, let's call him Jose (not his real name) came to us from one of the most violent suburbs of Mixco. He had a strong determination to live for God and to serve Him with all his heart. He was an inspiration to everyone at school, staff as well as students. His father had difficulty holding down a job, his mother had been murdered and his brother-in-law, had been kidnapped and murdered. He had an older brother who was in jail, yet his attitude and enthusiasm for life was something to behold. He had a strong prayer life. A leader among his peers, he was brilliant in his studies, so much so that he worked hard in his own time to learn to speak English. At the end of his first year of studies in Arkansas, the Dean of Students wrote to our administrator to commend the W.C.V.T.C. for its good preparation of Jose. He is now back in Guatemala serving as an official in one of the many foreign embassies in Guatemala City. Others have gone on into business management and computer technology. One of our students who took dental hygiene as her specialty, continued through university to become a dentist, she will be graduating in 2017. Due to the regular devotional periods held through the week at the school, where the students are encouraged to worship the Lord through music, many now are leaders in their home churches. Some are headed for full time ministry. I read somewhere that while it's possible for us to know how many seeds there are in an apple, knowing how many apples are in a seed is something that only God can know. Try to imagine first of all, how many apples a fruit farmer receives from the first harvest of a young tree. I don't know how many years an apple tree yields it's fruit, but I do know that the hundreds of thousands of apples from just one tree, were somewhere inside that one apple seed when it was planted. And so we must keep on working for the Lord, just as the evangelist was working who had the privilege of leading Dr. Billy Graham to the Lord those many years ago. Only God knows the full effect upon the world and upon His eternal kingdom that we as His servants will have, when we intentionally invest our time, talent and or treasure into another young life. Everyone who sponsors a child or gives towards missions or gives an offering in his or her local church, is paying forward with the limited amount at their disposal, which holds potentially eternal dividends when given in faith that God will use it for His glory. We often think of God's family growing by addition but when the Holy Spirit is involved it becomes multiplication with exponential growth.

Remember I mentioned earlier that when we first arrived in Papua New Guinea, all we had to our name was $60.00. The Lord had provided me with a great job, thanks to the machining skills I picked up in South Africa, and within six months, Pauline and I were able to establish the new 'Lifeline' office in Port

Moresby and join two other couples in planting an Assemblies of God church in the Gordon's suburb of Port Moresby. Our job is just to do what we know we should do. The rest we must leave in God's hands.

Every move we have made along this fascinating and exciting journey has meant a new beginning for our two children Simon and Tracy. They took to life in the tropics like fish to water. This was where they both started school. David, the part time missionary who we had teamed up with had already started a Sunday school. Simon and Tracy joined right in and loved it. This was when we discovered Simon's good sense of rhythm. We held the Sunday school in the Gordon's primary and junior school building, where all the kids were sat at individual desks. During the singing of choruses, Simon would beat the rhythm on the top of his desk, he was very good at it. So it wasn't long before we bought him a set of bongo drums, which he played from that point on. Tracy loved to sing and she would swing from side to side as she sang. She was always quick to volunteer to come out to the front and sing a solo. I can see her now, five years of age, standing at the front of the room, swaying in her long colourful dress singing, "Here comes Jesus, see Him walking on the water He will lift you up and help you to stand…." It's wonderful to know that over forty years later they are both still loving and serving the Lord.

At that young age, Tracy knew no fear. We were visiting one of the villages when she caught sight of a Papua New Guinea tree house. This was a traditional treehouse that was there basically for the sake of tourists. The nationals don't need to use these defense houses anymore because the tribal wars are virtually finished. Trust me when I tell you that Tarzan wouldn't want to be up this tree. It stands about thirty feet in the air, just one slender trunk and a few branches up at the top. The only way up and down was by way of a kind of rope ladder with pieces of wood for the steps. We were enjoying a chat with the folk from the village when someone pointed to the tree house. We turned round to see Tracy already half way up the ladder. She was so determined to enjoy being in a tree house that nothing was going to stop her. Pauline's motherly instinct kicked in immediately and courageously started to ascend the rope ladder. She got up to about 15 feet and made the mistake of turning around. She froze and slowly started to descend. I don't like heights, but I knew that if this was going to end well, I had to get up there before Tracy missed her footing and came down the fast way! When I reached the top, the tree was swaying back and forth a couple of feet and hot on my trail was Simon! Holding on to the rope with one hand and Tracy with the other, we all started down the ladder. Simon first, then me, then Tracy. She would have stayed up there if I had let her. She loved every minute of the adventure. On another occasion we were enjoying a paddle in the ocean when Tracy yelled "A snake". It had literally swam right between her legs as she was snorkeling, it was a poisonous black and white striped zebra snake. We thanked the Lord for keeping her safe that day.

What a wonderful privilege it was for Pauline and me that the Lord would direct us to live and work in P.N.G. We supported ourselves with good steady jobs. Pauline working as an administrative secretary in a local business, during school hours, while I worked in the sciences workshop at the University of Papua New Guinea. In the evenings we worked in the Lifeline Bible Correspondence office, along with several other volunteers. On Sundays we helped with Sunday school as well as Sunday morning worship services. Most of the people attending church were young men and women who had come to the capital city to attend one of the many colleges. There was the University, the Teacher's College, The Police College, Nursing school as well as other training facilities for industry.

For the people who were coming from villages where missionaries were working, it was easier for them to adapt in the city. Mainly because they were coming from homes that had accepted the Christian faith and values that we taught in the church. But for those who were still believers in animism and worshiping the spirits of their ancestors, life in the city was confusing and complicated. I remember one young man who had been attending our church all year and it seemed was enjoying it. But he grew more serious as the end of the school year drew near. He was from the Sepik district on the North of the island where many of our Christian young people were from, but he was from a village that still rejected the Gospel of Jesus Christ. The difficulty he faced this particular year was that on his arrival back in the village, he was scheduled to go through the initiation ceremony in becoming an adult. He came to see me along with some of his friends to ask my advice as to what he should do, especially in regard to various ritualistic activities that he would have to participate in, back home in the village, which due to their sexual characteristics ran contrary to Christian values. I answered his heart wrenching questions as carefully and graciously as I could, but on his return to the village, we were never to see him again.

But for every sad story, there are many great and happy stories. Take Johnny for example, he was the very first P.N.G. national I spoke to. He was part of the small welcoming group that were waiting at David's house on our arrival. I remember climbing out of David's combie van, walking up to him, shaking hands and slowly saying, "Do you speak English?" Johnny gave me a huge smile and replied in perfect English, "Well I try". You can imagine, this became a regular joke from that time on.

Johnny was also from the Sepik district. He spoke his own village language, he was fluent in English as well as the national language of Pidgin English. It was estimated at the time that P.N.G. had around 600 dialects and languages from both the Polynesian and Melanesian sides of the island. Extremely primitive groups of people were still being discovered in the early 70's. Especially in parts of the Highlands in the interior, over near the border with Irian Jaya. Johnny had been raised in the village of Maprik which had had the benefit of good Christian missionary work throughout the area ever since the end of the Second World War. Excellent schools had been established as well as churches. Television had not yet come to P.N.G. so to stay in touch with the outside world we would listen to Radio Australia and of course the international service of the B.B.C. Local stations did exist but we tuned in to the international news stations most of the time on our short wave radio.

I do remember listening to a local station though, when the new 'House of Assembly' self-government session was being broadcast and hearing one of the new members reflecting on how far the progress of development had come. He was speaking to the House of Commons when he said, "...I remember as a child, nibbling on a human finger, which was a real treat to us kids ..." I believe the discussion at the time was one of trying to work out how to set appropriate laws that would take into consideration traditions of tribal warfare and cultures of pay-back that had been entrenched for millennia.

There were several interesting cases in the news at the time. One was where a party had gone out of control and a man had died in the melee that ensued. A new police outpost had been set up in the area; so now the sober party goers were afraid of being found out and punished. They thought they would solve the problem by cooking and eating the body. They had buried the bones under the house. Houses there are usually elevated on stilts to avoid snakes and flooding. Somehow the bones were discovered and the 'evidence eaters' were jailed.

Another case I remember very clearly happened shortly after 'self-government' had begun. A member of the House of Assembly was on official business some distance outside Mt. Hagen in the Highlands district. He was there to gather information for a report he was working on and was accompanied by a colleague from the Department of Health. As they were driving along what then was just a dirt road, they hit a young pig. The young pigs along with the dogs, run in and around the villages and have no road sense at all. Consequently you have to drive defensively just in case a child or one of these highly valued animals jumps in front of you. Generally speaking the people of the Highlands are friendly and hospitable. But when they feel wronged in any way, their first reaction is to hit back, similar to the Old Testament law of 'an eye for an eye and a tooth for a tooth.'

The two government officials felt they should stop and try to make things right with the villagers, but this was the worst thing to do right at that moment because within seconds, several enraged men came running at the bewildered officials and hacked them to death with machetes. Later when tempers had cooled down, these men were arrested and later sentenced to just a minimum sentence due to the issue of fairness, with the understanding that this deeply inbred culture needed time to catch up with western styles of government law and justice. Johnny was a student at the university majoring in Business Management. On graduating he was quickly snatched up by the Department of Posts and Telegraphs. Rising through the ranks he was promoted from one excellent position to another, now holding the position of International Director. He was still working for the P.N.G. Post and Telegraphs when he later stopped off in our home city of Edmonton, Canada. At that time, it was the middle of winter in the early 1980's. We picked him up at the airport and upon exiting he was so excited about seeing snow for the first time in his life, he fell into the snow making the image of an angel. Throwing it in the air and allowing it to fall on his face. Pure joy, coming from something that we take so much for granted.

It was such a privilege to be in Papua New Guinea at that particular time period. We were able to witness first hand, a country emerging out of what was effectively the Stone Age and coming to grips with modernity. When we arrived there in 1972, P.N.G. was still a protected territory under the oversite of Australia. It had been slowly developing as a protectorate since the end of World War 2.

16th September, 1975 was to bring independence to Papua New Guinea. The year prior to 1975 was called, the year of 'self-government'. It was during this time that government positions were scheduled to be filled as much as possible by nationals. It would still take a few years to bring these trained individuals on stream but we were confident that with brilliant, sharp young men and women such as Johnny and his wife to be Cecilia, all would be well in the not too distant future. It was no surprise to see Mr. Michael Somare being sworn in as the first Prime Minister of P.N.G. He too was raised and educated in the Sepik and was able to help this brand new, independent nation take its place in our fast moving family of nations.

It's nothing unusual for young people in the country regions to want to be going to the big city to find work and adventure, but here we were seeing literally hundreds of youths flowing into Port Moresby to go through the various schools of training. Knowing where these young folk had come from and the adjustments to modernity they would make, they would never go back to live in the village and stay with their families again. And how hard it would be on the families back home. A new beginning for a whole generation.

I'll never forget how hard it was for Simon and Tracy when after finishing middle school in Guayaquil, Ecuador, they had to go to boarding school in Quito, the capital city, because there were no high schools that functioned in the English language in the coastal city of Guayaquil, where we lived. Again they were faced with a new beginning, only this time it was away from home. They had never been away from mum and dad before, so now they were being called upon to be brave in a way that was new to them and they were brave.

This all happened following our time in P.N.G. I had acquired a position with the British Overseas Development Agency as technical support with a team of engineers cooperating in the development of a Polytechnic in Guayaquil. We were serving the Lord through the establishment of the Lifeline Gospel Literature ministry in our spare time.

Simon adjusted to boarding school relatively well. Tracy had a much harder time of it. We would fly them down to our home in Guayaquil once each month and were permitted to call them by phone, twice each week. Most times went well but toward the end of their schooling in Quito, it was obvious to us that dorm life was causing more harm than good. The young dorm parents didn't seem to have the necessary skills in compassion and caring, so the crunch time came when we had to take them both out of the dormitory and place them into alternative accommodation. Thankfully my contract was coming to an end so it was only a matter of months and school in Quito was finished.

We take so many things for granted in the comforts and organized framework of western society and culture. Two humorous stories come to mind that illustrate this reality. We had recently acquired a Boxer puppy and was needing to graduate him from just drinking milk to eating something more substantial. Pauline set out one day to buy some puppy dog food. Not too complicated, right? Wrong. Shopping isn't too difficult these days even if you can't speak the language, because you can just point to what you want, pay the price of the item and it's yours. At this early stage of our stay in Ecuador, Pauline didn't speak much Spanish. She tried looking for the pet food section but there didn't appear to be one. So in her usual inimitable way, she tried talking to the girls in the supermarket. No one understood her. They called others over to see if they could help this increasingly determined foreigner, to no avail. As a last resort Pauline began making puppy dog noises while at the same time motioning her hands to her mouth, with the additional eating noises. They got it! And when the hysterical moment died down, they all said, "No hay!" meaning, there isn't any! What a surprise to find out that in the late 1970's, pet food didn't exist as a particular product in Ecuador. Pets were fed what their owners were eating or what they prepared especially for them.

The second story is not for the faint of heart. Or should I say, the faint of nose. From time to time, new team members would arrive from Britain to replace those whose contracts were completed. Those of us who remained would drive them around and show them the area until their vehicle arrived. Pauline was giving the latest wife a tour of down town Guayaquil. Traffic was always bumper to bumper, moving slowly and on this particular street even more delays due to the construction of a high rise office block. There was no air conditioner in the car, so the ladies had the windows open. The temperature was somewhere in the lower 30c which was normal at sea level at the equator. Remember that this was an English car with the steering wheel on the right side. The scaffolding being used at the time was large lengths of bamboo about four inches in diameter. These were simply tied together with string. Vertical pieces and horizontal pieces with an occasional diagonal piece. Up and up they would go. Ten, twelve stories high. We can only surmise as to why the construction worker felt it necessary to do what he did, perhaps he was up against a deadline or the trip to the ablutions was too far; but just as Pauline was pointing out the unique type of bamboo scaffolding, he let go his load from way up top and the poop was a direct hit on the open window sill of the car. Hot and fresh, falling as it did from a great height, it splashed, ricocheting into the front of the car across the steering wheel and dashboard with no mercy on the occupants. You can only imagine the squeals as these two English ladies frantically seeking after some paper or cloths of some kind in order to recover some semblance of decorum. There was none to be found in the car. Nevertheless our time in Ecuador was good and enjoyable and God willing was fruitful for the Kingdom. But when the time came for us to consider another move, we were ready.

Chapter 11

SETTLING IN CANADA.

W e were now at another crossroads. It was the summer of 1981. All through that final year of my contract with the British Overseas Development Agency, we had been earnestly seeking the Lord for further direction. Because we were self-supporting as part time missionaries with the Lifeline Gospel Literature and Bible Study follow up, which was now continued through one of the Assemblies of God churches in Guayaquil, any extra money that we had, during that time, went towards printing and postage costs. Knowing God's faithfulness, we simply made our decisions based on the knowledge that He would guide us to where He wanted us to be, that He would take care of us in the meantime.

We had been asking the Lord where we should go especially with Simon and Tracy being in their early teens. We could go back to England or Australia, or even perhaps to Canada.

We wanted our next move to be a stable place so that as a family, we would not only have somewhere to call home, but also live where there would be good potential for schooling and later for job opportunities for Simon and Tracy. Already having lived on three mission fields, we were fully aware of how easy it can be for parents who are missionaries to relegate their children's needs to a fairly low level on the list of life's priorities. We didn't want our offspring rebelling against God because of parental neglect in the name of 'service for God'. Pauline and I knew full well that God had given us these wonderful kids and that His smile would be upon us as we considered His divine will for their lives and futures as well as for ours.

Time was going by and my contract was almost finished, when a husband and wife team of doctors came down to the Politech from the University of Alberta in Canada. They had come at the invitation of the Rector, to give advice on the latest techniques in technical education. As they were unable to speak any Spanish, we invited them to our home for dinner. Drs. Karl and Frances Puffer were delightful guests to have in our home. Unbeknown to them, they came into our lives just when we were anticipating hearing from God. We had been asking the Lord where we should go. And now we had this lovely couple, in our home, saying without prompting, "You should come to Alberta, it's a wonderful, peaceful place for you and your children". I couldn't believe my ears. I knew it was

Karl speaking but deep down in my heart I also knew I was hearing from my Heavenly Father. During their brief stay in Guayaquil, Ecuador, we invited them over again but this time to glean as much information as possible about life in Alberta, Canada. After some further intensive prayer and fasting, we applied to the Canadian Consulate in Quito for our 'landed immigrant' status. We did not know it at the time but this process was a slow one. Once we started the process, well before the end of my contract, we just had to wait.

The next thing that happened was the end of the school year for Simon and Tracy. It was good to have them home now, knowing that they wouldn't have to return to the situation in Quito. The following thing that occurred was the end of my contract with the British Government. This also brought an end to our contract with our accommodation. We now had just a matter of days before having to move, when we received an invitation to dinner from a friend from church, whose husband owned a large business in Latin America. As we were enjoying our Ecuadorian meal, the husband said he had heard we were in need of somewhere to live temporarily, he had a vacant furnished apartment that we could use for free if we so wanted. God is always faithful with His children even though he includes unique, last minute type testing's of our faith.

We continued checking with the Canadian Consulate office, but they just repeated, "Check back in two weeks". Several 'two weeks' went by which now turned into months. This extension of our stay in Ecuador created a new series of challenges for us. We now needed extensions of our I.D. cedulas, which everyone needs in order to function legally. Also, extensions of our visas in order to simply be in Ecuador as foreigners. We kept waiting and praying, praying and waiting. During this time we received word that the business man needed his apartment for the following week. We were so grateful for being able to stay in it and we thanked him sincerely. I had sold our car in the meantime, so we were still able to cover all our costs during this transition.

By faith, we moved into one of the nicer hotels in the centre of Guayaquil. It had a pool and the room had a television. This was a little easier for the kids, as the apartment was sparse, hot and no T.V. so we all had to entertain ourselves throughout the sweltering 30°c evenings. The family soon got tired of listening to my 'campfire' stories. We had been in the hotel a little over a week, when we heard the exciting news that our application had been approved and we could travel to Canada as soon as we wished. This news came to us the day of Charles and Diana's wedding, 29th July 1981. How we enjoyed seeing it all televised, then with tickets in hand, we set off the following day for the land of our future home, Canada.

Heritage Day in Edmonton, Alberta will always remain a special memory to the four of us. 3rd August 1981. We had arrived at the airport the previous evening to be greeted by Drs. Karl and Frances Puffer, who took us to their home, offering us a place to stay until such time that I found work and a place to live. Karl and Frances were the only people we knew in Edmonton of course, but God was at work establishing a pathway for us, in every step that we would take. Karl had already arranged an interview for me for that first Monday morning. The manager was in his office even though it was a provincial holiday. The interview went well, he wanted me to start work the next day. But he was considerate enough to allow me a few days to find a place to live and get mobile again. A month later Simon and Tracy were in school, we were settled in the Millwood's area and already enjoying the ministry of Pastor Wally Riehl at the Millwoods Pentecostal Assembly.

It wasn't long before we were all fully involved in the life of the church, especially in the area of small groups under the leadership of Pastor Gary Taitinger. Simon and Tracy did well at their new school and participated in the youth activities at church. Pauline was blessed with a good permanent position at a local Doctor's clinic. And so, we settled into life and lay ministry, with a contentment to see our kids established and to continue seeking the Lord for more of Himself in our lives as we served Him in and through this growing church.

Always in the back of our minds was the thought that somewhere down the road, the Lord would open the door of opportunity for us to venture out once more and serve Him by becoming an answer to someone's prayer.

We had been patiently waiting for Simon and Tracy to at least be ensconced in their higher education with some clear direction in their lives, before considering making another move. Being forward planners though we were always checking what possibilities were out there for us to consider as a married couple in our late thirties, early forties.

It was six years later that Pastor Wally Riehl went home to be with his Lord and Saviour as mentioned in chapter one. Pastor Gary, now the senior pastor, later brought me on staff as an associate where both Pauline and I enjoyed eight full and fruitful years of service.

May 1995 saw us on our way to Guatemala. Yet the school didn't open until January 2007. Eleven years of carefully walking with the Lord as He took us through the gauntlet of having to deal with the constantly changing government bureaucracy, followed by the exciting, miracle-strewn process of seeing the building going up and experiencing the joy of hosting the opening ceremony of the William Cornelius Vocational Training Centre. Some might be wondering how we came to choose the school's name. This story in itself would rank as more, clear evidence of what God had in mind from the start.

Chapter 12

THE CORNELIUS STORY

I t is always a joy to talk about what it was that brought us to the decision to name this Christian technical school; The William Cornelius Vocational Training Centre. For while it is a great privilege for the school to carry his name, there was no way, at the time of choosing it in 1997 for us to know how significant this very special name is for the country of Guatemala, and the testimony of Jesus Christ.

During the long, drawn out process of applying for the land, after presenting our proposal to the mayor of Mixco, we were then directed to the Ministry of Education.

From here, our proposal would go from one ministry to another and back again. This was what took such a long time. Things slowed down at the change of government and went even slower when I refused to offer bribes. Our whole file was misplaced at one point, forcing us to start the process all over again. At times I would take Harold with me, a young Guatemalan who spoke English, other times Hector Aragon would come along just to make sure I was understanding the instructions they were giving. About six months into the second go round of paper chasing, we were instructed to provide a name for the institution. They required the name of an honourable person who had passed on. A name that was not already being used but had the reputation of having been a person who made a difference in our world. We had an informal advisory Board at the time and they asked me to provide a name. The only name that stood out in my mind was William Cornelius.

We first came into contact with Pastor Bill in 1982. As chairman of the new missions committee in our home church in Edmonton, I had the privilege of communicating with him and eventually meeting him when he would visit the churches across Canada. As a young man he had been in ministry as a pastor in Saskatchewan, marrying his beloved Lillian in 1953 and answered the call to the foreign field of Kenya in 1955. Bill and Lillian's ministry was very fruitful through their church planting and building of schools, which were just beginning to develop in that part of Africa.

In 1965 Bill was appointed as Field Secretary which meant that he would be working with missionaries from Kenya, Tanzania and Uganda as well as national pastors and churches. In 1980 he was elected Executive Director of

Overseas Missions of the Pentecostal Assemblies of Canada. This was a very challenging position. Under his gracious and encouraging leadership he would have the privilege of seeing new mission fields opened up and witness God's blessing around the world as he travelled to many different fields. On 17th December, 1992, while preparing to set out on another missionary journey, Bill was suddenly called home and went to be with the Lord of all missions. Bill was single minded in his love for Jesus and the work of the Kingdom. He was always a great encouragement to those involved in any aspect of missionary work, even to those engaged in mission's promotions at the local church level. He was a humble person who looked upon all people as special in God's sight. He believed in simplicity and honesty and went ahead in faith to see projects through even though there were many obstacles and the way did not always seem clear. The theme of his life was, 'be positive, trust God, don't worry about tomorrow, God is sovereign'.

So while it is true that God has used several men to influence my life, Bill was the only outstanding one that had gone home to his reward. The choice then was not a difficult one. We would name the school, The William Cornelius Vocational Training Centre. This was July 1997. No longer just a 'school project' we now had a distinct name. We had written to the family of course, his wife Lillian and children had graciously agreed to allow the school to be named, in his honour.

And so for Pauline and me, with the added assistance of Edna and Hector, it was back to the treadmill of trying to expedite the growing file of official paperwork, as it seemed to be moving at the speed of a Canadian glacier. The Spanish language on the other hand is spoken at break-neck-speed. So these thrusts into the labyrinth of government offices helped me tremendously to catch the rhythm and cadence of this beautiful language, much quicker than the hours spent one on one with my language teacher. Most words in Spanish end with a vowel, so to an English speakers ear, a sentence can quite easily sound like one long word. For Pauline and me, learning to speak Spanish was unquestionably hard, but a whole lot of fun.

The Spanish word for 'sins' is 'pecados'. You can imagine the reaction as Pauline was sharing with her tutor one day, how grateful she was to the Lord for taking away her sins. But instead of saying 'pecados' she said 'pescados' which are fish'. I was telling someone about Dexter our dog, but instead of saying 'perro' which means 'dog', where it is necessary in pronouncing this word to roll the double 'rr', I lazily said 'pedo' which means 'breaking wind'. Laughter certainly breaks the tension at times like this and sure keeps a person humble.

Years now, were going by as our 'expediente' (file) was moving through its course. We prayed and fasted for this process to speed up and come to an end. Only later were we able to see why in actual fact, this part of what God was doing was necessary. It was growing our faith. It was preparing churches across Canada to come alongside us with plans to send volunteer work teams. Others were being moved by the Holy Spirit to come on board financially so that when we would send out a memo informing of a particular need, they were ready to respond.

We needed extra time in order to get the engineering drawing translated into Guatemalan code. It was these same drawings that the Engineering Ministries International had so graciously provided during this waiting period. It also gave us the opportunity to study and prepare many lists and documents that we would need later for the starting of a technical high school. It gave us the advantage of being ready ahead of time for most of the challenges we would meet.

It was early afternoon one Saturday in December of 1999. We received a phone call from Edna, our associate in the ministry who would later become the director of the school. She was laughing and crying and trying to tell us something all at the same time. Edna was speaking English, but we still couldn't figure out what she was saying, nor why she was so excited. She was calling from a building in Antigua called the 'Capitania General de Guatemala'. Antigua is a beautiful quaint city about one hour west of Guatemala City. It is the original capital city of Guatemala. The Capitania General de Guatemala was until recently, the Police Station of Antigua.

Built in the 1500's, it was the original police headquarters of the old capital city of Guatemala. Standing on the steps, looking out across the main plaza from the front of the Cathedral, this imposing, multi arched building takes up the entire south side of the plaza on the left hand side. Edna was attending a special, 'Year 2000, Turn of the Century' conference, hosted by the Guatemalan Evangelical Alliance. The speaker was Virgilio Zapata Areyuz who in 1982 had authoured 'The History of the Evangelical Church in Guatemala'. The subject of his message on this particular Saturday morning pertained to the courage of the Christian in standing up for what he believes, even to the point of giving his life.(Phil. 3: 7-14). The example he used was taken from the above mentioned book, pages 4, 5 and 6. The following is a translated excerpt from these pages:

William Cornelius, Irish born in Cork, came as a sailor on the 'Minion' ship, of the John Hawkins expedition. He arrived finally in Tampico, Mexico. His true name was John Martin, son of Peter Martin, sexton of the Cork cathedral. According to Dr. Gonzalo Baez Comargo in his well-documented work; 'Protestantes Enjuiciados en Iberoamerica', it appears that William Cornelius was the first protestant to arrive in Guatemala. Right after the first collective process (taxation process) of 1568 in Mexico City, he went to Guatemala where he established his professions as both Barber and Surgeon. In 1574 he was arrested and charged as a 'heretic'. Refusing to deny his (protestant) faith, he was sent back to Mexico to be tried under the Mexican inquisition. He was sentenced on March 6, 1575, in the Chapel of San Jose de Naturales at the convent of San Francisco to be executed for believing that we receive salvation by grace, through faith in Jesus Christ alone. He was later hung and his body was burned along with garbage from the San Hipolito market. This market used to be where the present day Badillo Street and Colon intersect in Mexico City. We know very little about the activities of William Cornelius in Guatemala during his years there between 1568 and 1574, yet it is only logical to deduce that for his protestant character and the fact that he was deported from the country as a heretic, his testimony and his personal life and words, certainly spread through the neighbourhood to reach the ears of the ecclesiastical authorities and governors of the capital city of Guatemala. Thus William Cornelius was tried in the local 'commissary' and extradited to Mexico. The author concludes that the William Cornelius case is typical of the happenings in Guatemala during the sixteenth, seventeenth and eighteenth centuries. There were many who were put to death for their faith during this difficult period of the Inquisition but according to available records, these took place after that of William Cornelius. (Quote by permission).

In order to comply with the requirements of the Guatemalan Ministry of Education at that time in 1997, it was great to hear that the family had consented to the school, being named for their husband and father, William Cornelius. And now, in the December of 1999, we were hearing for the very first time, that the first protestant Christian had been arrested for heresy in Antigua and taken to the 'Capitania General de Guatemala' where he was officially charged after which he was marched on foot, all the way to Mexico. Little did we know that not only did the Lord plan for us to honour our own, Canadian William Cornelius, but it was in His plan also to honour the William Cornelius of the sixteenth century, who had valiantly given his life as the first martyr for his faith. That men and women, boys and girls are not saved by being born to a religious family nor are they saved through good deeds and piety, but all men who come to Christ must come through faith, believing in the atoning death of Jesus on the Cross of Calvary. That He died for all mankind there. But only those who realize that Jesus was suffering and dying for them and being willing to repent of their sin, asking the Lord for forgiveness, can a man be saved. This then, is the exercise of faith, believing that salvation has now come to us only by the loving, merciful grace of God.

No wonder Edna was so emotional. The conference she was enjoying, was taking place in the very same building that that Irish protestant was imprisoned before being forced marched to his death!

Salvation hasn't changed, nor the need for it. Though the church has grown in many parts of the world, so has resistance to the truth of God's Word. Even within the Christian Church, it has become stylish to act and sound like the world, even to where using such words as sin, judgement and hell are being discouraged in order to attract visitors. If Jesus came to speak in these churches, what words would He be trying to avoid? He knows what lies ahead for the skeptic and the unbeliever. He knows the inner workings of the human heart, He created it. I've always found it interesting that when the Lord walked and talked with man, women and lots of children, He talked more about judgement and hell than about heaven and grace. How can it be that we have so many leaders in the work of God who appear to want to be like Jesus, but find it uncomfortable talking like Him?

Resistance to the truth of the Gospel has never been greater than it is today. Christians are being persecuted, driven from their homes and murdered in many places in our confused world. Paul tells us in chapter 6 verse 18 of his letter to the believers in the church at Ephesus that we should be interceding on behalf of our brothers and sisters in Christ. The early church knew what it was like to be surrounded by hostile neighbours and communities. Paul reminds us all, especially those of us in the western societies who have all the modern comforts, that we should pray for all the saints everywhere. We don't know when the Lord will return for His Bride, nor do we know if persecution and deprivation will eventually come to our towns and cities. One thing is sure, the Gospel of Jesus Christ has always been and still is, an offense to the world around us. When I was a child in Sunday school, we used to sing about Daniel. 'Dare to be a Daniel, dare to stand alone, dare to have a purpose firm and dare to make it known'.

Have I, have you got the courage like the Irish William Cornelius to stand up for what you believe, to the point of death?

The Lord Jesus, long after His death, resurrection and ascension back to His Father in heaven, speaking through John the revelator to the church in Ephesus said

'....He who has an ear, let him hear what the Spirit says to the churches. To him who over-comes I will give to eat from the tree of life, which is in the midst of the Paradise of God'. Rev. 2:7

To each of those seven churches, Jesus gives an individual assessment (Rev. 2 and 3). The church in Philadelphia was maintaining acceptable standards and received a good report. Some of the others were working hard to keep up, but several, we can see were a complete mess. Every one of these high-lighted churches are given a conditional promise. Blessings will be given to those who overcome. Someone who overcomes, doesn't give up. An overcomer is a person who remains faithful to the Lord. A church that overcomes is a church that stays the course, holds its banner high and doesn't back down in the face of adversity. The enemy of the Church is the Devil. Jesus has conquered Satan but he is still on the loose. They say that all publicity is good publicity. This adage however is not the case with Satan. He prefers keeping a low profile so that he can attack unsuspecting Christians when we least expect it. This is why Paul provides us with an excellent overview of the believer's daily defense strategy in Ephesians 6: 12-18. Concluding with the description of our one and only offensive weapon: The sword of the Spirit which is the word of God.

It is helpful to remember that each and every piece of armour is describing the Lord Jesus:

The belt of truth. (v14) Jesus said in John 14:6 "I am the ......truth".

The breastplate of righteousness (v14) Paul tells us in Philippians 3:9 that Jesus is our righteousness.

Wear spiritual footwear called the gospel of peace (v15) Jesus is our peace. Philippians 4:7.

The shield of faith (v16) Faith makes us overcomers through Jesus 1 John 5:4-5.

The helmet of salvation (v17) Our salvation is in Christ Jesus. Romans 1:16

The sword of the Spirit which is the word of God (v17) Jesus is the Word of God. John 1: 1, 14.

In this spiritual warfare that, like it or not, every follower of Jesus is enlisted in, we should all take courage knowing that Jesus is our victor over Satan and that He has given to us everything we need to stand strong. He has promised that

He will never leave us nor forsake us, even until the end of the age. Oh that we might be able to say like Paul "For me to live is Christ, and to die is gain!" (Phil. 1:21). What a marvelous attitude this is for anyone whose mind is at perfect peace with God.

But let us not forget another Cornelius who was a first; Cornelius the Roman centurion who we read about in the book of Acts chapter 10.

The Holy Spirit inspired Luke to provide us with the whole story of the beginning of the fulfillment of the promise of God to Abram, as we read it in Genesis 12:1-3.

Now the Lord had said to Abram:

"Get out of your country, from your family and from your father's house, to a land that I will show you. I will make you a great nation, I will bless you and make your name great, and you shall be a blessing. I will bless those who bless you, and I will curse him who curses you, and in you all the families of the earth shall be blessed".

Jesus the Messiah did come to the lost sheep of Israel and all the Jews who believed on Him were indeed saved. The disciples for instance, and the thousands who were added to the church on the Day of Pentecost, all were Jews. It would take a sovereign move of God to include Gentiles in this new Church. As Paul puts it, 'For He (Jesus) Himself is our peace, who has made both one, and has broken down the middle wall of separation...... (Eph. 2:14). Paul is probably referring to the wall that separated the Court of the Gentiles from the inner court of the Temple. Jews considered Gentiles as sub-human and totally unworthy of fellowship. So we see the hand of God in bringing about the fulfillment of His great plan, to pour out upon all mankind His grace and favour. That His only begotten Son's death on the Cross would suffice in cancelling all our debt of sin towards God and, His judgement towards us.

The time was right. God sent His messenger to speak to Cornelius. He was a Roman centurion. A tough leader of men. A Gentile who feared God and helped the poor. God will always respond to that combination in a person who is seeking truth. God didn't need to have Peter come in order for Cornelius to be saved, but in God's sovereign wisdom, it was necessary for Peter to experience seeing the grace of God coming upon Gentiles. It took one visit from an angel for Cornelius to get things happening. It took a vision with triple shock treatment to grab Peter's attention and ready him to agree to go with Cornelius' servant. Were it not for the intervention of the supernatural, conducting every facet of this historic event, the church leaders would never have wanted to include Gentiles into the church at all. God answers prayer. We see in Acts 10:2 that

Cornelius prayed to God always and immediately verse 3 tells us that he saw the angel. Then verse 9 tells us that Peter went on the housetop to pray, followed by what I call, three hard smacks upside the head to soften his self-righteous, legalistic attitude toward people who didn't matchup to his inbred community and traditions. Salvation was and is to be for all men everywhere who desire to follow Jesus Christ.

The promise to Abram (later called Abraham) was coming to pass with the salvation, baptism in the Holy Spirit and in water, of Cornelius and his household. Thanks be to the Lord God Almighty, who has lovingly swung open the doors of heaven to all who will enter in through the finished work of Jesus in His death, burial, resurrection and ascension back to the Father where He now waits to welcome all members of His family, both Jew and Gentile.

What a wonderful story is wrapped up in this name of Cornelius. Most recent our own Pastor Bill Cornelius whose memory is still greatly esteemed throughout the Pentecostal Assemblies of Canada. Then the Irish William Cornelius who became the first martyr for his faith in Guatemala. Then of course the Roman soldier of Acts chapter 10, who was the very first Gentile to believe that Jesus was the Son of God and gave His life, becoming the Saviour of the world to all who will believe (John 3:16).

If Edna had not attended that conference, it's quite possible that we might never have learned just how significant the name of the school was to Guatemala. But these serendipitous encounters with people have occurred many times through the planning and building phases. Each one helping the process along, adding richness and colour along the way.

2007, The William Cornelius Vocational Training Centre was operating well. We had an academic director along with a full slate of teachers and instructors. All had now fallen into a smooth routine. The school would continue growing bigger each year, bringing new challenges to the focus of our prayers.

CHAPTER 13

SCHOOL LIFE.

During our first year of operation, responding to the needs that surfaced grew exponentially. Before opening day it was just the needs of our local team along with our national workers. Now, we had a dozen teachers, administration and maintenance staff to consider as well. But our focus which we were all in agreement on, was the students. Young lives that God had given to us to bless, to teach and to shape; characters with huge potential. Personalities with new hope and expectations for the future. Coming out each morning from generational poverty and hearing words of loving encouragement; not only of math and science and grammar, but about God's love and grace and faithfulness. It wasn't hard to prove to them that God is a God of miracles and still answers prayer. They were surrounded and enveloped in an atmosphere of praise and thanksgiving. Everywhere they looked they saw the evidence of the abundance of God's provision. They were learning in a building that was itself, a miracle.

During those first couple of years of school, construction jobs were still being finished on the third floor, even while the students were in classrooms on the first and second floors. Students of the first year were all in Computer Technology, but the second year students had the choice of going into the computer stream or into the Dental Hygienist stream. So now, along with praying that the driveway and car park all around the school might be covered with 'adoquin', which is a flat cobble stone arrangement, we were also praying that these precious young men and women would be covered with the protection of the Blood of Jesus as they traversed some of the most dangerous areas of Guatemala City each morning and each afternoon.

It was noted that one of the students hadn't come to school. After he missed the second day, his friend informed the administrator that he couldn't come to school, as he did not have money for bus fare. The equivalent at that time in Canadian money would have been less than ten cents. This story touched the heart of a work team member who had come with a team from Edmonton. He decided to leave enough money with the school to cover the student's bus fare for his remaining time at school. So many of these wonderful work teams that came down to work at the school did so much more than just exhaust themselves doing construction work.

It became apparent that some of the students were falling asleep in class. Our first thought was that they were staying up late at night. But on digging a little deeper, we discovered that they were coming to school with empty stomachs. Some students were from single parent homes and if the parent was sick or out of work, there was no money for food. This triggered another heartwarming project from a couple who were team members from Ontario. They felt very moved about this sad situation; on going back home, with heartfelt love and thoughts toward the students, they sent the initial money to start us off, in supplying breakfast each morning for the students who needed one. This was then carried on by one of our Canadian missionary couples, once they became aware of the need. Many of our wonderful work team members began sponsoring a student after having seen for themselves the extent of the need and how powerfully such an investment can change a life.

One morning we were discussing how God answers prayer for those who believe. This was during the English language class. One student said that we needed to pray for a T.V. and V.H.S. recorder unit in order for the English teacher to be able to show them a teaching series on Video tape. We ended the class with special prayer that God would grant us the ability to buy a T.V and V.H.S. unit.

I was in my office around lunch time when a visiting pastor from a church just south of Edmonton, came in to tell me that his church Board had given him $1,000.00 to buy something for the school during his two day stay. He asked if we had an immediate need in the school. I told him what had transpired that morning and together, we went to purchase a good sized T.V. and V.H.S. recorder. I'll leave it to your own imagination as to how the students reacted to this news. God is so good, all the time.

Another B.C. team gave us two day's work as they were just passing through. They noticed that the kitchen still needed a double door. They asked what the cost would be, had a whip round and gave us the money for the doors. The Lord used this same method to provide the music class with a guitar and amplifier. It cannot be over emphasized how gracious and kind have been our churches across Canada. We would have named them all, but the risk of overlooking one, prevents us from doing this. Sufficient to say that we had multiple groups coming from British Columbia, Alberta, Manitoba, Ontario, Quebec and Newfoundland. Every group played a vital part in the construction and preparation of the W.C.V.T.C. including the three groups of volunteers that came from the U.S.A.

Work continued all the way through to 2009. The new cobble stone driveway was completed and a beautiful sheltered picnic area was built, in order for the many students to eat their lunch, shaded from the direct sun and rain. By the third year of operation, an 'Electricity Workshop' was added along with courses in design and graphic art. Work was also started on the laboratory workshop for the latest area of training – that of Dental Technology. Such technologies as these, in tandem with Dental Hygienist and Computer training have already provided excellent career possibilities to several hundred graduates. Each new career that has been brought on stream represent huge investments on the part of donors who quietly go about their work quite anonymously across Canada. God knows who they are and the reason they have done it. All deeds of kindness small and great, God records for future reference (Rev. 14:13). Not all the students who have studied at the W.C.V.T.C. will turn out to be bright, shining lights for God's Kingdom, but many will. This is the part of the overall strategy that we must leave with the Holy Spirit. After all, this is His work. At the front of the central waterfall and garden feature, there is a bronze Bible in the open position. On the page to the left, it shows the original promise text God gave to us as a word to the students taken from Psalms 113: 7-8.

He raises the poor out of the dust,
And lifts the needy out of the ash heap,
That He may seat him with princes.
With the princes of His people.

The Psalmist is himself quoting from Hannah's prayer of thanksgiving found in 1 Samuel 2:8. God had answered her prayer in giving her a son Samuel, who she then dedicated back to God. God raised up Samuel to be a great leader to the nation of Israel, both as a priest and as a judge. Later ushering in the era of the Kings who would then rule over Israel. First anointing Saul, then David, whose earthly lineage would eventually bring the Son of David, the Son of Man, the King of Kings and the Lord of Lords. Jesus, the very Second Member of the Trinity.

A more wonderful blessing we could not bestow upon these great, young people as they would begin to ponder and seek the Lord for what He had in store for them and their future.

On the right side of the bronze Bible, the raised lettering spelled out those profound words of Jesus to His disciples:

"I am the vine, you are the branches.

He who abides in Me, and I in him,

bears much fruit, for without Me you

can do nothing......" John 15:5

This scripture is a solemn reminder to all the staff, teachers and administration, that if we would be fruitful in the work and Kingdom of God, it behooves us to abide in the Vine. To draw from Him as the eternal source and resource of life and power. That we as branches might be used of God to be conduits of truth, joy and peace, coming from the Lord, passing through our own hearts, minds and spirits, flowing into the young fruit placed in our care. Only eternity will show how fruitful has been the harvest.

After a couple of rainy season had come and gone, it became obvious that something would have to be done about the flooding in the central patio and landings of the school. For when the skies would open up, the torrential rain would pour into the open plan of the school and all the walkways around the courtyard would be swimming. Water would then run down the elegant stairways into the library on the second floor and the foyer on the ground floor. It is so easy to slip on wet, granite floors, so it was agreed to find a not too expensive way to cover the patio with a transparent roof. We decided on a segmented dome design that would keep the water out while letting the light in. So with the help from a church in Ontario, which sent a donation in lieu of a work team, the dome was built and in place long before the rainy season returned, to test it out. It worked! We were now able to hold events even when it rained.

Much was happening during our final year in Guatemala. The youth groups of the P.A.O.C. churches were initiating a special fund raising project all across Canada. They organized huge concerts with the goal of financing the drilling of wells in the developing world, and especially the countries with P.A.O.C. missionaries on site, for the sake of managing the work to make sure it was done properly. We were still having our water trucked in each week to fill our water tanks, so to receive the news that the W.C.V.T.C. had been chosen to have a well drilled on site, was wonderful news.

The drilling for our 'Water for Life' well, started on the 1st May, 2009 and finished with Kelvin Honsinger, director of E.R.D.O. being present and actually switching on the pump on the 11th August the same year. We thanked the Lord for providing us with a good supply of clean drinking water and we thanked the young people of our church constituency for their vision and labour of love; not only for Guatemala but also for the many other localities and villages in many other places around the world where water is so desperately needed. Those of us who have grown up in the west expect to be able to go to a tap or faucet and have water splashing out simply by turning the handle. Yet there are millions around the world who have never experienced such luxury. How wonderful of our Lord, to make the 'water of life' available to all who would drink of it. In the Gospel of Matthew 10: 40 and 42, Jesus speaks to those who would receive Him and to those who will help the needy. He says:

"He who receives you receives Me, and he
who receives Me receives Him who sent Me.
.....And whoever gives one of these little ones
only a cup of cold water in the name of a

disciple, assuredly, I say to you, he shall by no means lose his reward".

On another occasion we see Jesus offering the 'water of life' to a Samaritan woman.
(John 4:10, 13 & 14) He says:

".....If you knew the gift of God, and who it is who says to you, 'Give Me a drink', you would have asked Him, and He would have given you living water".
".....Whoever drinks of this water will thirst again, but whoever drinks of the water that I shall give him will never thirst. But the water that I shall give him will become in him a fountain of water springing up into everlasting life".

Attending the W.C.V.T.C. the students now have the joy of receiving fresh water to quench their physical thirst. But through such periods in the course of their school week, as morning devotions, Christian ethics, Friday afternoon praise and worship and special spiritual emphasis events, they are provided with rich, blessed moments, where the peace and love of God's holy presence may be experienced. It has been at times like this that so many have entered into a personal understanding of what it means to invite the Lord Jesus into their hearts. To drink for the very first time, the living water of eternal life. Our physical thirst can be quenched temporarily, with a soothing cup of fresh cool water, but only the sincere opening of the palate of our souls can our spirit drink in the regenerating, eternal water of life, that comes to the human heart, when we realize our need and ask Jesus to grab the reins and take control of our lives.

All the difficulties and problems that missionaries and leaders of ministries go through for years on end, are happily accepted, when fruit is finally seen, growing on the ends of those branches. It is simply for us to remain and abide in the Vine. God is the faithful Gardener and desires good fruit.

Looking back over the various stages of the W.C.V.T.C. becoming a reality, it would be understandable for some to think that it was all graft and hardship up to the time of the school's opening. The truth is, every step in the process was more than just a bridge to the next phase. God was working His divine plan. People's lives were being changed. Many of the work team members would share their testimonies at the closing fellowship gatherings which were held the evening before returning to Canada; how that coming away from home and the various situations they were struggling with, they were better able to sense the presence of God and hear His voice comforting them and bringing them peace. Some teams gave the first hour of each work day to a brief sharing of devotions followed by a personal prayer walk. These times were spent in quiet reflective prayer, where the volunteers were free to walk or sit wherever they wished. Some would walk the perimeter, seeking the Lord for His blessing upon the school grounds. Others asked the Lord to station His angelic forces to guard the property, keeping the forces of evil out. Much prayer went up for all the future students and staff members who would one day be coming to work and study in this special place. Testimonies were shared from some who had met the Lord in a very powerful way while on their knees in the middle of the building site. Later testifying that their spiritual life had been reignited during their stay in Guatemala.

Several of the roughly six hundred volunteers who joined work teams over the eight year period, working on the school, actually came to know the Lord as their own personal Saviour while on the worksite. How loving and gracious of the Lord to work His eternal purposes and have them come down to Guatemala, out of their environment and routine, to here confront them with their need of a Saviour. Others were baptized in water on different occasions. All were glad they had come, that they had come to work and give but in so doing, had received the blessing themselves. When a person comes with the right attitude, even at their own expense and using their vacation time, it isn't long before they realize that what they are doing is for the Lord. Making a sacrifice as unto Him, brings dividends that ripple on into the future. As mentioned earlier, one common reaction to the sovereign move of the Holy Spirit is tears. Tears of repentance, tears of joy, tears of finally letting go all resistance to the wooing of the Spirit, tears of gratitude, tears of relief. All such experiences dissolve doubt and cynicism. The soul bursts with new faith and determination to follow and serve the Lord. The Lord's closeness reinvigorates our very human excitement in the thrill of knowing that God will never leave us nor forsake us. And for those who very stoically prefer to trust in God's faithfulness towards us without the need to show any emotion whatever, I wonder what your position will be at that first, grand meeting when all who believe, will stand in the throne room of God, and see Jesus step forth?

Now, almost ten years of school life has gone by. We are told to 'occupy till He come', as Jesus alluded to His absence between His first coming and His eventual return (Luke 19:11-27). He shared this important information in a parable as He was on His way to keep His historic appointment with His entrance into Jerusalem on a donkey. Fulfilling the prophecy of Zechariah 9:9 which speaks to His first coming. The above mentioned parable then, helps us to understand and be patient in waiting for His sure return. (See Luke 19:12-15). We are told to work for the Master until He returns. We are not told how long He will be away but we are assured that He will come back. Investing in the work of God is what this parable teaches us to do. Whether this is through supporting your local church or other local ministries, or helping send workers overseas as missionaries or simply helping to finance the myriad practical endeavours for the sake of Christ, we must work for the Master while it is day, for a time is coming when we won't be able to do anymore work for God. One thing we can all do is share our own testimony.

Soon, I believe, the Father will say to the Son, "Go, bring My waiting people home". We see in Matthew's Gospel chapter 24: 36 to 44 that no one knows when Christ will return but we are warned to be ready, "......for the Son of man is coming at an hour you do not expect....."

It is vital that all men everywhere (this includes all women of course), hear the good news that Jesus came to bring. So many say that they will leave it till later. There are two deadlines, either of which, if we meet before accepting the Lord, will preempt any future possibility: The first obvious one is death. We don't know the date of our own death, so being ready in our spiritual life in advance of this date is vital. The second and less obvious one is the Lord's second coming. Most evangelical Christians believe that the 'rapture' of the Church will take place shortly before the Lord's second coming. Either way, it behooves us all to make prior preparation for eternity. We do this by inviting the Lord Jesus to come into our hearts and accept Him as Lord and Saviour. Revelation 3:20 Jesus says:

"....Behold I stand at the door and knock. If anyone hears My voice and opens the door, I will come in to him and dine with him, and he with Me...."

Here, Jesus is speaking about the door of the heart. Not the physical muscle that pumps blood, but the centre of the human soul. Our intellect and understanding of all that we see and hear in the world around us. When we open our heart to the Lord who is Spirit, He makes our spirit alive. No thanks to Adam, our spirit lost its awareness of the glory of God and effectively died. But when we come to Jesus, we are given a measure of faith to believe through prevenient grace, and our dead spirit is made alive in Christ. We become regenerated by the same power of the Holy Spirit that raised Christ from the dead. Bringing to us the free gift of eternal life through Jesus Christ our Lord.

A special joy we will carry with us was to see the Canadian team members working alongside our national workers. Neither being able to speak each other's language yet obviously communicating with each other. One ingredient that made this possible was humility. Guatemalan people are characteristically humble, especially those of the ladino and Mayan folk. They were always ready and willing to learn something new from the many highly skilled construction workers from Canada. Our worksite supervisor was tremendously experienced in all areas of construction so it was truly gratifying to see how well he worked both with our national workers and with the Canadian team members. But having said that, it was always a treat to watch the Guatemalan 'albanils', (builders) building and plastering walls and ceilings using their simple basic tools, producing such high quality workmanship. Then later, to watch such loving relationships developing between team members and students. Many students seeing their sponsors returning each year to watch their progress, encourage them and bless them by being present at their graduation. Some are still in touch, long after graduation.

Our commitment was to remain at the school until we felt it could be run quite adequately without us. Edna the administrator was doing a wonderful job during our final year there both from the point of view of providing good administrative oversight, but also from the equally important spiritual aspect. Transitioning through a leadership change can be very difficult but Pauline and I truly thank the Lord for Edna who has been giving such good leadership to the W.C.V.T.C. since the beginning of 2009.

The William Cornelius Vocational Training Centre's very first graduation ceremony began at 3:00 pm on Saturday 24th October, 2009. Twenty four very excited students graduated that day. It was a historic event for the many who packed the multi-purpose hall, but for none more than these precious students, whose lives would never be the same again.

There was a whole array of guests in attendance. Parents and families of the graduates made up most of the crowd; but at least a third of those present were sponsors and special guests who had come from across Canada as well as the U.S.A. Several of the original E.M.I. engineers were present, now able to see some of the fruits of their labour. The graduation ceremony was followed by a celebratory banquet held in the beautiful central patio, which was adorned with lights along with the sound of the rippling central fountain in our ears. Each graduate had their own named table specially reserved for their family and sponsors. But there were so many attendees that tables were also prepared along the second and third floor landings. It was a wonderful day of smiles, relief, hugs and picture taking. Our excellent maintenance staff stayed behind to do the clearing up and setting up again in readiness for the next day. Sunday morning came around early. Rosa Alicia's tourist buses were ready and waiting outside the Tikal Futura Hotel, to take our guests to church at 9:00 am. Many had never been to the new, mega church 'La Fraternidad', so we chose to take them there. It is an independent Pentecostal church, seating for fourteen thousand. Worship there is always a joyous and moving experience. Pastor Jorge is a seasoned man of God who commands unusual levels of respect, not only from the members of his congregation but also from the highest levels of government. With around ten thousand people in attendance on any given Sunday morning service, it's quite understandable that they would have over four hundred volunteers working the car parks along with ushers, greeters, and a prayer team, and the top notch musicians who come to serve God's people each week.

It is an amazing thought to take in, that Guatemala ranks as one of the poorest countries in the western hemisphere per capita yet it hosts five or six mega churches in and around Guatemala City. How is this possible? I believe this small, Central American country is experiencing a wonderful outpouring of the grace of God upon it. First because it honours Israel and secondly because there is so much crime and corruption, the people of God are active in prayer and in sharing their faith. It is also worth pointing out that the majority of the population don't have the many distractions of the world to consume their time as we do in our affluent society, nor do they have the disposable income that causes so many to allow sports and entertainment to squeeze out and compete for our time.

Following the worship service at 'Frater', we all had lunch together at the picturesque 'Cabana Suiza' the Swiss Cabin restaurant, after which we made our way back to the school for our special celebratory time of giving thanks to the Lord for all He had done in bringing us to this momentous occasion. There was great resounding praise lifted up to the Lord, with leadership from one of the local churches. Several of our own students were playing their own instruments during this truly sacred time. How precious was the sense of the presence of the Lord. Rev. David Wells, our General Superintendent of the P.A.O.C. was the special speaker and special it was. His message spoke first to the crowd; then to the students and the challenges that lay ahead for them, reminding them that God would be going with them. Then his message focused in on Pauline and me in regards to our assignment in Guatemala being completed and that we were releasing the leadership of the W.C.V.T.C. over to Edna. He then turned to the students saying, "We released the Slaters to you, will you now, release the Slaters back to Canada?" They all solemnly answered in the affirmative. He asked the students to gather around us in a circle and then prayed a powerfully anointed prayer over the students and then over Pauline and me. Most thought that the formalities were over at this point. They were not. We had one more, very important part of the service to perform.

So much of God's leading and guiding in our lives and in the lives of many others was irrefutably obvious in the miraculous way this marvellous school had come into being; we felt it would be appropriate to publically come before the Lord, approach His throne of grace, to ask that the anointing of the

Holy Spirit that we had felt, would now come upon Edna in her role as Administrator and leader of the school. Pauline and I walked up to the rostrum and asked Rev. Gary Taitinger to also come up to the front. What a treat and thrill it was for us to have our home church Pastor and friend attending this special and blessed occasion. Once the three of us were gathered on the platform alongside the students, we called Edna to come forward, to turn, and face the congregation. Edna was not aware of it, but we had had a beautiful royal blue mantle made for the occasion. Pauline took out the mantel from behind the podium and caped it over Edna's shoulders. At this point Pastor Gary prayed the blessing of heaven down upon Edna, that she would be constantly walking in God's will in giving leadership to this precious gift of God to the people of Guatemala. He then continued in prayer that Pauline and I would be led to what the Lord had in store for us on our return to Canada. It was a powerful moment for everyone there. Edna kept the mantle on, even throughout the fellowship meal that followed. It was a glorious transition. Later that week we said our final goodbyes to all our friends at the school. Our music teacher was also a pastor in one of the local churches, he had agreed to give spiritual oversight and council at the school both to the students and the staff.

We were ready now for the moving company to come, bringing to a close the fourteen years of loving service that had so powerfully impacted our lives in Guatemala. On arriving at the airport, very early in the morning, we had a surprise. There was Edna along with her son, standing to greet us and say goodbye, with her 'mantle' around her shoulders. Precious moments.

We arrived back in Edmonton on 1st November, 2009. Friends opened their home to us and provided us with a car, so that we could take our time seeking the Lord for what He had for us to do on our next assignment.

CHAPTER 14

A SENIOR ASSIGNMENT.

That there would be another assignment was obvious to us, mainly because we knew we were in no financial position to be able to retire, even though I was now sixty four years of age. All through our life's journey we were determined to do what the Lord directed. Most of the time, we operated with minimum resources, knowing and trusting that the Lord would always provide for our needs. He always did. And now that we were no longer working as missionaries assigned to a particular geographic area, this didn't mean we were no longer being cared for by our Heavenly Father; even though we no longer received a pay cheque. We rested in the knowledge that God had something more for us to do. Something that would suit our gifting's as well as our age group.

For several years we had been talking about what we hoped would be the kind of ministry we would like to be involved in. I knew I had to find a full time position that would provide us the opportunity of saving for retirement and we both had a strong inclination towards working with seniors. So, on returning to Canada, while we were waiting to hear from the Lord we decided to spend that first winter in Kelowna. We loved Edmonton and felt very much at home there. But, we were not looking forward to dealing with the cold weather, after fourteen years in the 'land of eternal spring', a nick name for Guatemala. We were overjoyed at the offer from some friends, to let us stay in their Kelowna coach home for the winter of 2009-2010.

While there, we earnestly sought the Lord for what He would have us do next. So how do we earnestly seek the Lord for His guidance? Do we wring our hands constantly worried and fretting that we need to hear something A.S.A.P.? No. Do we chant and repeat the same prayer or mantra over and over again hoping God will be sufficiently impressed to answer? No. Do we spend four to five hours in prayer each day trying to make up for our usual, poor prayer life? No. There's nothing wrong in spending hours in prayer, but only if our motive for doing so is acceptable to the Lord. The power of prayer is based on faith. And faith is only functional if we know who it is that we are putting our faith in. If we don't know the Lord Jesus personally, we would have no confidence that our prayers will be answered. The Lord Jesus is a person. Yes He is God. He is God the Saviour. He died for you personally and desires a personal relationship with you and with me. So when we come to Him, we're coming to a person who we know. Someone who we spend time with, not just a sugar-daddy up there who we come to when we want something. So again, how do we earnestly seek the Lord?

We determine to spend quality time with Him. Then it becomes obvious, He already knows what we need. I love to spend times of quiet reflection on His word, His will and His ways. Often as I'm reading from God's Word, regardless of what book of the Old or New Testament, something will stand out, touching something in my spirit that will cause me to stop, read it again, spend some time pondering what it means, what it might be saying to me as to what is going on in my circumstances right then. This is one of the many ways that we receive a nudge from the Lord when we are seeking His face. It is during these times of waiting on the Lord that we are best tuned to hear His voice speaking to us. Not only through His marvelous love letter to us, His word, but also through listening to the preaching of His word. There are also dynamic gifts of the Holy Spirit available to us. Prophecy is not dead, it is a method designed by God which He uses still, in order to communicate something special to those who He has decided to speak to in this particular way. Tongues and interpretation is another of God's wonderful ways of communication to us as His people. If we only think of these things with negative responses, so much of what God may be saying to us is missed. His last words before being arrested were that He no longer calls His followers servants but friends (John 15:15) Jesus tells His followers in John 14:13-14 "......whatever you ask in My name, that I will do, that the Father may be glorified in the Son. If you ask anything in My name, I will do it". In John 15:16 Jesus says; "....You did not choose Me, but I chose you and appointed you that you should go and bear fruit, and that your fruit should remain, that whatever you ask the Father in My name He may give you....". Then we see in John 16:23-24 Jesus repeats; "And in that day you will ask Me nothing. Most assuredly, I say to you, whatever you ask the Father in My name He will give you. Until now you have asked nothing in My name. Ask, and you will receive, that your joy may be full...." Jesus then says it again in John 16:26-27. "....In that day you will ask in My name, and I do not say to you that I shall pray the Father for you, for the Father Himself loves you, because you have loved Me, and have believed that I came forth from God..." Jesus wants us to get to know Him personally and it is when we come to know Him and have a close, ongoing relationship with Him that we can then earnestly seek Him for His guidance.

We felt in our hearts that we should do some fasting along with our praying, this we did for eight days. During this period the Lord was speaking to us through His Word and through circumstances; telling us that we were where He wanted us to be and to continue trusting Him. He related to us about a wheel–that can go quickly or slowly; though we might not see the wheel moving, it surely was, be it slowly. This was such an encouragement to us. We felt Him close to us. It was a time of rest and recuperation, especially from the physical point of view. Spiritually it was a delight for both Pauline and me to be able to sit under the excellent ministry from the Pastors of the Evangel church, enjoying fellowship with the believers there.

Each morning following a devotional time, I would get my head into a study book. We were both busy trying to keep our minds active as well as our bodies so that when we received our directive from the Lord, we would be ready. But still, nothing coming from the Lord. Our time allotment in our accommodation was coming to an end so we decided to take the opportunity to visit with family in Edmonton, Alberta and continue our drive to visit family in Hamilton, Ontario also. The evening before we left Kelowna, we were at the church on the last day of a week-long seminar on the ministry of the Holy Spirit. I had already left the auditorium when Pauline called me to come back to hear a word of encouragement from a doctor friend of ours with whom we had been enjoying good, spiritual fellowship during our stay. He said that he didn't usually have visions and dreams but the Lord had spoken to him the night before, saying that he should tell us the following, "That we were on the right path and that we would go full circle". He said that was all the Lord had said to tell us. We were pleased to know that we were on the right path but we had no idea where going 'full circle' would lead us. Nevertheless, we trusted the doctor because we knew him to be a very godly and spiritual man.

27th March 2010.

Leaving the next morning, we took our time driving once again across this great country of Canada. While in Kelowna we had written to the district offices of the P.A.O.C. in British Columbia and Ontario, hoping and praying that a position would open up where I would be able to serve in an associate pastoral capacity, believing that the Lord expects us to do what we can, while leaving to Him, the things that we can't. Once in Hamilton we stayed with family and friends, trusting that in His time, the Lord would open a door of opportunity. Another three months had now gone by. Much prayer and fasting was the order of the day. Funds were now getting low, which actually helped us to really focus on listening for the voice of God. We were hoping to find a church that was in need of a senior's pastor but the Lord had other ideas. He was working behind the scenes, we knew this, mainly by the regular promptings we were receiving from our daily devotional readings. There was also the absolute assurance that this awesome, wonderful

God who we serve, had never ever let us down in the past and wouldn't be letting us down now. Even though we couldn't see what lay ahead, we did know that we were walking in God's favour. I'm not suggesting that God has favourites, for He is no respecter of persons, meaning He doesn't bless some while turning His back on others. He loves us all equally, and His grace is towards all men. But not all men love and obey God, which causes them to miss the blessings of God's favour.

We were enjoying the loving hospitality of our friends in Brantford, Ontario as we patiently waited on God. Then, on the 7th May, we received an e-mail from Pastor Gary asking if we would be interested in a part time position, pastoring seniors at the Shepherd's Care facility in Kensington, Edmonton. I thanked him for the thought but told him that I was looking for a full-time position, after which he responded by saying that they wanted someone full time, but he thought I was looking for a part-time position. E-mails went back and forth during the month of May even as prayers went heavenward. We felt that the Lord had opened a door for us and that we should go through it.

As was the custom, each morning Pauline would check our e-mails. This particular day she mentioned that someone called John was praying for us – as the subject was John Pray. On reading the contents of the letter, it became clear it was John Pray, the President and C.E.O. of The Shepherd's Care Foundation who had written the letter. He was asking us if we were interested in the position, use your imagination as to our response! We were flown to Edmonton, with accommodation and transport provided in readiness for our interview. Following the interview with John along with several Board members, it was agreed that we would begin serving at the Kensington campus on the 1st August, 2010. Pauline would work part-time and I would work full-time, as Pastors of the Kensington Village, Shepherd's Care facility.

During the month of June, many things had to happen. We said our goodbyes to our daughter Tracy and family and to our good friends John & Joyce in Brantford, Ontario and drove back across the prairies to Edmonton. It was good to re-unite with our son Simon and his family as well as the many friends we had there, spanning over 30 years. Two very special friends with the gift of hospitality, Jack & Marlyn provided us with a temporary home while settling in once again in the capitol city of Alberta.

Moving day was 2nd August, 2010. We had bought furniture, due to arrive on the 4th. Then, thanks to the missions department of the Evangel Church in Kelowna, our boxes of personal effects arrived on the 5th. They were able to keep it in storage for us on arrival from Guatemala, until such time we had an address for them to be delivered to. So many have been truly kind and helpful towards us for which we are deeply grateful. Passing through times of transition can be some of the most difficult, but the love shown by the family of God is one of the brightest reflections we have of the face of Jesus Christ.

It was on Sunday the first day of August that we were introduced and had a chance to speak to the congregation of God's people at Kensington. And with this began another fruitful assignment from the Lord, using what He had given to us in order to bless others in trying to make the part of the world where He had placed us, better.

There were many hours of orientation and adjusting to this new environment. While the majority of people living at K.V. (Kensington Village) are independent residents, many are in need of some assistance each day, many are long term care and some are being cared for as they struggle with dementia and Alzheimer's. So while the specialized health care professionals provide the expertise needed in the various levels of senior care, all staff members including those in pastoral care are required to be aware and cooperate as one compassionate and loving team, serving the seniors in our care.

Ours of course, was to minister to their spiritual needs in particular but we quickly became aware that ministering to these senior adults was equally as great a blessing to us as it was to them. I made it clear from the start that I was an ordained Pentecostal minister but that I loved and respected the diversity of communities and traditions within the great family of God. One quick survey showed us that we were enjoying fellowship with followers of Christ from such church groups as the Salvation Army, Anglican, United Church, Roman Catholic, Baptist, Pentecostal, Nazarene, Reformed, Eastern Orthodox, Mennonite, Ukrainian Catholic, Church of God, Christian & Missionary Alliance and Lutheran. Some were skeptical at first, others a little tentative about this new preacher, but once the newness wore off and they realized that I was serious about the responsibility of preaching the Gospel in a clear and simple manner, the congregation began to grow. We were truly an interdenominational group of believers.

There were many living at the Kensington Shepherd's Care who still attended their own local church and of course a large but unknown number who had no church affiliation at all. And while there were a few who kept well away from any 'religious' activity, most were respectful, knowing that they were living in a facility operated by a Christian organization.

The Shepherd's Care Foundation was first conceived in 1970, following a breakfast meeting with a group of 28 men from the Southside Pentecostal Assembly in Edmonton. They were concerned for the welfare of their aging parents, that they would have a facility where they could feel comfortable and safe and be able to continue to enjoy being in the Christian environment that was such an important part of their lives. Shortly after, the men (along with their wives), mortgaged their homes and built the Shepherd's Care Manor on 28 Avenue in Mill Woods, Edmonton, Alberta. It has grown from there to now operating six beautiful campuses, as a not for profit organization, providing accommodation for roughly 1700 seniors.

It was a privilege, along with the full-time Chaplain, Rev. Fred George, to provide the residents with a full slate of Christian activities ranging from Sunday worship services along with mid-week Bible studies to informal fellowship times with tea and cookies.

Together we also provided quarterly memorial services to remember those who had passed on most recently. Highlights of the year were Christmas and Easter, when we would have a choir from one of our local churches come with their inspiring and always joyful cantatas. Other activities included a weekly prayer group where we had special prayer emphasis for any resident who was sick or in hospital, for the leaders of our country, for our children and grandchildren and the administrators and staff members of the S.C.F.

Hospital visitation was very important with sometimes taking a whole day to visit with our various residents, who for different reasons would be in one of the eight hospitals or recuperation facilities available to the people of Edmonton. People of any age group can be at their lowest when sickness comes their way. But our senior adults are that much more prone to developing a physical weakness or even falling and breaking a limb, than are the younger folk. So to be regular with a visit, with a brief reading from God's word, an encouraging chat and a prayer of faith, can certainly assist a hurting person in their recovery. We would visit them in their homes and respond also to a request for a visit and immediately try to comfort a bereaving spouse. Quite often a person would come to our office for counselling or special prayer. We were open to all comers of course, not just those who attended our church services.

Staff members were also welcome to come with their questions and needs, no strings attached. We made it our goal to share the love of Jesus to all, regardless of their cultural or religious background, knowing that for many in our multi-cultural society, we might be the only Jesus they would ever see. And when you have the love of Jesus in your heart, loving others isn't difficult.

Looking back on the five years of service at Kensington, several things come to mind:

Great worship services.

We were ministering to people that were born in the 1920's and 1930's. This was the generation that was giving leadership to God's people when Pauline and I were growing up. We cut our teeth on the pews in front of us (I can still taste the varnish) and on the gloriously inspiring hymns of the Christian faith. Most of which were theologically correct. We would sing some choruses but this 'inter-church congregation would come alive when Iris, our magnificent pianist would strike those anthemic chords, giving so many old, wheezing lungs their weekly work out. It's hard for our younger generation to understand perhaps, why anyone would enjoy singing such old fashioned words and music, but to people in their 70's, 80's and 90's and even a couple over a 100, these hymns of rich worship allow the quietest and most conservative believer to express their love and adoration to the Lord their God. And having grown up ourselves in a singing church, we could easily relate and thoroughly enjoy worshiping the Lord in this manner.

My preaching style was more that of a teacher. My goal in my sermon preparation was the 'spiritual formation' of the congregation. That no matter where in God's holy word I was preaching from, the aim of the message was to enlighten and strengthen some basic tenet of the faith in the hearts of the listener. Steps of salvation were paramount, with Jesus and His finished work of the Cross remaining front and centre. Using texts alternately from the Old Testament and the New Testament, but always leading to a point of personal application of what it was the Lord was saying to us from His word. Tuesday afternoon Bible studies were more of an inductive style of working through a book of the Bible.

Altar calls were a regular and integral feature of our Sunday services, though due to limited mobility for so many as well as the church cultural mix, rather than call people to the front,

I would ask that all who would like to accept the Lord as their own personal Saviour, to please repeat this prayer after me:

> "Dear Jesus, I know that I am a sinner I know that
> You died for me on the Cross as my substitute
> to take away my sin. I now repent of my sin and
> ask You to forgive me. Come into my heart Lord
> Jesus, take control of my life. Thank you. Amen".

It was always a thrill for me to hear different ones praying this sinner's prayer. Often a person would come up to me following the service and thank me for explaining the 'Good News', telling me that they had attended church all their lives yet had never heard it like that before. My feeling about being given this opportunity to speak into the hearts of these precious seniors was that I should not miss a chance to lead a person closer to the Lord. And that if I was faithful in doing my part, the Holy Spirit would be faithful in doing His. For us, this assignment was a rescue mission. There are over fifty references in the Bible to Hell. Jesus in Matthew 5 makes it clear that Hell is a place that we should avoid at all cost. Paul in Romans 1 and Peter in 2 Peter 2 agree that doing things our own way will surely lead us there. I couldn't assume that everyone coming to our church services were believers who had at some point in their lives, invited the Lord Jesus into their hearts. All were well over the 'three score years and ten', and it was not unusual to hear that Mrs. A or Mr. B had passed away suddenly that week. Often I would wonder where the soul of that lovely lady was or where was Mr. B. today? We cannot know, where a person is at spiritually. Only God knows for sure. However, we can know and be sure regarding our own soul. The Apostle John tells us in 1 John 5:1.

> Whoever believes that Jesus is the Christ is born of God, and everyone who loves Him who begot also loves Him who is begotten of Him.

Then in 1 John 5:11-13 John says:

> And this is the testimony: that God has given us eternal life, and this life is in His Son. He who has the Son has life, he who does not have the Son of God does not have life. These things I have written to you who believe in the name of the Son of God, that you may know that you have eternal life, and that you may continue to believe in the name of the Son of God.

And so we see from scripture that we can know for sure that we are born of God, born again of the Spirit of God.

We received an urgent call one Saturday, from the daughter of a dear senior lady who wasn't doing well in hospital. She was a regular in church. A typical 'church goer' who you would never think twice about their salvation. Church was a priority for her. She paid close attention to the preaching of the word. Always had a pleasant hand shake and greeting. But as Pauline and I sat by her bedside, she carefully and slowly explained that she had never been sure that she was 'saved' and bound for heaven. We gently pointed her to such a scripture as John 3:16 and Ephesians 2: 8 -9 and Romans 6:23. Showing her that because of what Jesus did for us on the Cross, it is for us simply to believe, thank Him and receive the 'free gift' of eternal life. We can't do anything to earn it. As it says in Romans 6:23.

For the wages of sin is death, but the gift of God
is eternal life in Christ Jesus our Lord.

We then prayed together, that the Lord would bless her with a confident sense of assurance of her salvation. It seems that many of the older, faithful generation of church members, who have conscientiously devoted their time, talent and treasure to their local church and I am talking particularly about our classical church denominations, are shocked to discover that becoming and being a true believer, is more than just showing up and doing. If even after being a member of a church for fifty years, there is no personal relationship with the Lord, no desire to give heartfelt worship in gratitude for what He has done and showing only a cynical attitude to any talk of the near return of the Lord, why would anyone think that this represents a follower of Jesus Christ at all? Once again, it's a comfort to know that God is the judge and not ourselves.

One gentleman that we were visiting in the Royal Alexander Hospital was aware of his grave condition physically. In his late nineties, had recently lost his wife and had kept us at arm's length from the outset. But as we gradually got to know one another, keeping our visits brief and not too intrusive, he warmed up to us and began sharing his concerns and fears. I had been asking the Lord for an opportunity to see where he was spiritually even though I knew he had been a lifelong member of a national church. At an appropriate moment in our conversation, I asked him if he had ever asked the Lord to come into his heart. There was a pause. He was thinking. Then he lifted his head and looked me in the eye and said, "No I haven't". I asked him if he would like to do so. He said "Yes". We prayed together. He said, "Now I get it". He thanked us for sharing with him and we left the hospital. It wasn't very long after that special time with him, that he passed into the presence of the Lord.

Another gentleman diagnosed with lung cancer, was at the top of the list of people who complained about every little item on his agenda. He always appeared to be grumpy, yet willing to talk to us. He had been a heavy smoker and drinker all his adult life and knew that he was now suffering the physical consequences of treating his body so harshly.

Whenever we mentioned the love and grace of God he would become quiet and very respectful. His questions were clearly testing our responses to sin and forgiveness. He knew that we were not of his denomination and openly expressed his anger and disappointment that no one from his church had come to visit and comfort him. We suggested that he should be more considerate and forgiving, especially as he was probably considered a 'lapsed member' of his church. Each time we visited him in hospital and just before leaving his bedside, we would ask him if it would be alright to pray for him. After a while, we could see that he was becoming more spiritually aware. We prayed that he would know the touch of God upon him both physically and spiritually and that he would be at peace with God and man.

We were all aware of his serious condition, and that there was nothing more the hospital could do for him, so just before leaving him on that very special Wednesday afternoon, I asked him if he was ready for the question, he immediately said "Yes!" The question was, would you like to ask Jesus to come into your heart and be the Lord of your life? Again without hesitation he said "Yes I would". We prayed together a simple prayer.

We were all shedding tears of relief and joy. A few days later he was back at Kensington Village.

His whole demeanor had changed. When one of the administrators checked to see if he was happy with his food, knowing how quick he usually was with his complaints, he said,

"Don't worry........I'm a different man now". A couple of weeks later, he asked the nurse to please get him his small travelling case from off the top of the cupboard, after which she asked, "Where are you going?" To which he replied, "I'm going home", pointing his boney finger heavenward. Not too long after that, he did. No more mister grumpy, he quietly and peacefully slipped away into the very gracious presence of his heavenly Father. We've all heard the cynical comments around the expression 'deathbed conversions'. Such negative thinking can only come from a person, who are themselves, spiritually bankrupt.

Anyone who has opened their heart to the Saviour could never ridicule such a vital concept. One day, when those who at this last moment on earth have accepted the Lord, as the One who opened heaven's door to them and are now themselves home in heaven, these will be the ones who will be able to seek out the thief who accepted Jesus as the Christ, as his Messiah, just before he himself died on his cross. He might not have been on a death bed, but he knew he would die that day, before sundown. What will this man answer to the question

"Was it worth it?" After gazing around at the indescribable wonders of heaven that will be his for eternity, he might remind his inquisitor to consider the alternative. The thief on the other side of the Saviour, who mocked and scorned the Lord, had the same opportunity as the first thief, but threw it away. This decision of all decisions that a person will make in the course of his or her life, is the absolute most deadly serious decision they will make. You will be in the same situation as one of these two thieves. Both were sinners, as are you. Both made a decision, as will you. God won't make it for you. He will however judge the outcome of your decision. He sent His Son Jesus to be your substitute, dying for your sin. By not accepting that Jesus willingly came and died to take away your sin, you will receive the judgement you deserve for all your unconfessed sin. But if you repent of your sin before God and receive His gift of eternal life, your sins will be remembered no more. The alternative is the worst, endless existence you can imagine multiplied a million times. So, let me tell you, death bed conversions are as valid as any other miraculous conversion.

One such example comes to mind with a really delightful man who would come to Kensington Village every day to visit with his wife. He had a wonderfully jovial personality but had no time for anything religious. Sunday afternoons would find him sat in the foyer waiting for his wife, often at the same time as I was speaking or singing during our Sunday afternoon worship services. One such occasion I had just finished leading a hymn when one or our receptionist came and handed a note to an usher asking to make sure I got the note immediately. It seemed urgent so I quickly read it. It said..."Pastor Alan, don't quit your day job!" signed.......For the sake of the story let's call him Harry. I read the note out loud to the congregation as they had all watched the drama unfold. The message I preach is always serious of course, but would always be interspersed with a humourous illustration or personal story, especially the ones that included Pauline's interactions with me. Harry certainly loved our chats and times of fellowship with him and his family but though he showed his love toward us so openly and though he sat so close to the preaching of the word of God, Harry would never set foot into the church auditorium. Several members of his family were believers and were praying that he would yield himself to the Lord. He was well advanced in years and eventually took a really bad fall, breaking his hip. This kind of situation is common with residents in their eighties and nineties and with the excellent techniques available to our hospitals and recuperation centre, it's not unusual to have our folks back up and walking again within a couple of months. But when Harry was taken to the emergency department, it was discovered that his heart was too weak for surgery. He was taken to the I.C.U. to see if they could stabilize him. But to no avail. He began to weaken fast. The family was called to his bedside. Because of our close relationship, we were called and asked to come and pray with him. He was conscious but couldn't speak due to all the tubes and equipment. By this time, Harry knew he was dying. His organs were shutting down and we knew he hadn't much time left this side of passing.

I chose a moment when most of the family were outside of the room. His Christian daughter remained in the room with us. I asked Harry if he was open to asking the Lord for forgiveness of his sins. He nodded that he was. I asked him to repeat my words in his heart and we prayed the sinner's prayer together. When I finished, I asked him if he prayed along with me, he acknowledged that he did, squeezing my hand and he looked straight into the eyes of his daughter across the room also. Soon after this, he slipped into a coma and never regained consciousness. His transition was a glorious one and we are looking forward to meeting him when it is time for us to go. There's one thing that cannot be disputed and that is, one hundred percent of us will die. And one hundred percent of us will be judged according to the decision we make about receiving or rejecting the Lord Jesus Christ. We have heard it said several times on these occasions by hospital staff that believers die well. One lifelong Christian lady was only minutes away from her home going when she was quietly singing along with Pauline and me, 'In the sweet by and by, we shall meet on that beautiful shore'. We were still singing the chorus when she stopped. She was already gone. Gone to a place that is sweeter than anything we could ever imagine. What a privilege it has been for us to be a part of the ending portion of so many people's lives down here on earth. But for a believer, what is considered the end down here, is only just the beginning of life eternal up there in heaven. Because of Jesus, death has been conquered and has no hold on a child of God. Though for those who reject the Lord, death will surely come and then it will be too late to do anything about it.

With the leadership help of Michael and Suzette, two of our volunteers, we held two sessions of the Alpha course during our tenure at K.V. This is the sixteen week, Christian based, informational course produced by Nicky Gumbel of London, England. It is open to anyone looking for answers to the great questions of life; who am I? Why am I here? And; is there more to life than this? Nicky eloquently, in his delightful British accent, goes on to answer these searching questions from the words of scripture while entertaining his listeners with both humourous and insightful illustrations mostly drawn from his own life's experience. Because this is non-intrusive, each weekly session ends with the listeners being challenged within their own heart to follow along with the closing prayer.

Consequently only the Holy Spirit really knows what changes if any, were taking place in people's hearts. But for us, the joy was that so many were interested in learning more about God. Again we were enjoying rich fellowship with members of so many different church communities. Reminiscent of what we understand from scripture (Revelation 5:13) that all who love and serve the Lord, will one day in the not so distant future, be able to gather around the throne of God; Jesus will be at the Father's right hand side and the multiplied millions who have yielded their hearts to the Lord throughout the ages, will be lifting their voices in rapturous worship unto Him who created us for a purpose, then made a way for us to be reconciled to the Father, bringing us home to be with Him forever. This truly is the greatest story ever told and the greatest romance ever realized and fulfilled.

One of the memories that we will carry with us from our time at Kensington Village is the daily treat we would experience just from walking down the corridors on our way to the Admin office or to the restaurant, or even just coming and going from our office on the third floor to our car below in the carpark. We would stop and chat with different residents along the way and also from time to time, just pray quietly with them as they shared their concern that day, mainly their health. Remember that the average age of the people at K.V. was 85. Old enough to be our parents.

This generation could still remember the 2nd World War and the deprivations that followed it. They were the ones who did all they could to help put our western society back on its feet.

They were farmers and railway men, trades men and women of any and all of the professions it takes to make a town and city. They are treasure troves of information. Always ready with stories about the 'dirty thirties' and forties. Stories about Vigny Ridge and military ships, about the 'fly boys' and 'war brides'. About migration and land clearing and building their first farm house. Stories about milking cows, collecting eggs and going to school in a buggy. Funny stories about breaking horses, baking bread and helping the neighbour bring in his harvest. There was never any talk of the latest cell phone or video game. These were people who wrote everything in longhand and were not afraid of holding an in-depth conversation. Pauline and I had great respect for those elderly, unsung heroes of our recent past. We also had the honour of officiating at many of their funerals. Yes, life goes on, things change and technology does make life easier. We certainly wouldn't want to go back to the thirties, forties or even the nineties, except perhaps for one glaring difference; respect for the word of God, for clergy, for police and for the law. Now it is 'cool' to challenge any and every symbol of authority, standard and value. To the point where even our leaders are showing relief at now being able to freely distance themselves from the God fearing values of the last generation. Of course God is still in control of His creation and will only allow rebellion to go so far before going to the next stage of His great plan for the world.

Another aspect of responsibility that presented itself to us, was the concern of the family members that we would, to the degree that we could, keep our eye on their mom or dad. It wasn't our job to be their caregiver and we certainly never interfered with those whose job it was. Nevertheless, it was one of the hardest things for us to see a sharp, vibrant, independent resident start to show the symptoms of dementia. The difficulty for their children was knowing when would be the right time to start to try making plans to ensure that their parent was being cared for at the right level.

I remember one distraught man coming over to me one day worried sick that his mother had totally lost her marbles. (His words) This happened during a transition period when the company was changing staffing arrangements and it was 'all hands on deck' for the managers and technical staff. He was upset because his mother had told him that "Yesterday Pastor Alan and Pauline were serving the coffee and tea in the restaurant". As he was telling me how worried he was, I said, "Yes, we were serving coffee and tea in the restaurant" He looked at me in disbelief and relief all at the same time. Pauline and I enjoyed many outbursts of laughter with the residents. We also shared in their times of difficulty and loss. It was a special privilege to join with those who knew and believed in the power of prayer and to know that so many of these precious seniors were including us in their daily prayer time. One of the reasons K.V. was such a wonderful place to work, apart from the fact that it is a ministry where the presence of God is felt throughout the building, is the administration staff. Pauline and I have worked in many different places, but we have never enjoyed this level of harmony before, amongst the managerial staff. The gifted person heading up this team was Sandra along with her assistant Nadine. They gave strong but gracious leadership to the dozen or so department heads. Everyone, a leader in their own right but working together for the good of the residents. This was truly a place of love and compassion both for residents and staff.

2014

The congregation at the Sunday afternoon worship services was steadily growing now to the point where if we were to grow any further, we would need a larger room. It took a lot of brainstorming on the part of the Board and Management but eventually it was decided to extend the patio on the third floor and build a church sanctuary that would accommodate a little over 250 souls. It was a new project in prayer. The cost for this church facility would have to be found outside of the Shepherd's Care Foundation budget.

We began as a church, to pray. Asking the Lord to help us in the raising of the funds. Everyone with an interest began to contribute. Residents and businessmen alike. The funds started to come in quite steadily, reached a little over half that was needed, then slowed down to a trickle. We were confident that this unique building project was inspired of the Lord and that it was a part of what God was and is doing in His world to give more pre-Christians an opportunity to hear the clear message of the Gospel and believe that Jesus came to give them life. So we regularly went to prayer and fasting, asking our faithful God to touch the hearts of those with a mind to give and a love for the work of God. We knew that there were many others who were praying also, especially those who were connected with the Shepherd's Care Foundation in some way. Hearts were touched, donations did come in, and faith was strengthened. Many who said it would never happen were now able to see for themselves that God hears prayer and when our prayers are in-sink with His will and purpose, He answers accordingly. God is faithful all the time and all the time, God is faithful. The church at K.V. is made up of people, who now have a really beautiful church facility in which to worship.

When Pauline and I were preparing to leave Guatemala, we knew we would need to find a job that would provide a livable wage, on our return to Canada. We did however, have a very special promise from God that the Holy Spirit had dropped into Pauline's heart during a service, whilst on furlough in 2004. God had simply said that we were not to worry because He would take care of us. We knew Him well enough to know He would keep His word.

We didn't find this position, God gave it to us. And though we only worked on this 'senior assignment' for five years, it provided the help we needed in order for us to be able to retire. It has been a wonderful place to work and serve and there couldn't have been a better situation for us to end the 'working part' of our journey. As seniors ourselves, we know that followers of Christ never actually retire from service. We look forward to seeing what the Lord has in store up ahead for us to do. We know that we will serve Him till either He calls us home through the transition of physical death to life with Him in heaven, or perhaps the rapture of the Church will take place sooner than later. In which case, all who are looking for His coming will be caught up together along with all believers who have died in Christ since Calvary. What a day that is going to be! No-one should risk missing it.

EPILOGUE

A s I sit and write, my gaze often drifts across the valley to the picturesque, spruce covered mountains that surround this part of Canada. Not far from where Pauline and I live stands a beautiful church with a magnificent, huge Cross reaching high above it. I love to see that Cross because it reminds me of the indescribable grace of God. That God the Father in consort with His Son, would devise a plan, conceived in love that would make it possible for sinful men and women to become acceptable before Him. God is holy and cannot look upon sin nor can He turn a blind eye to it. In His righteousness, God can only judge sin. An acceptable sacrifice for sin had to be pure and sinless, but no man or woman was ever sinless. This is why Jesus came. To be born a man yet still God. He was without sin and so was acceptable to God the Father as a perfect sacrifice. When Jesus willingly shed His perfect, sinless Blood on Calvary's Cross, it was sufficient to cleanse away all sin and its deserved judgement of all those who will believe.

This greatest event in all of history, created a new portal, leading to eternal life. A straight and narrow path, leading to heaven by way of the Cross of Christ, open now to all who believe that Jesus is God's Son and that He died on the Cross to take away our sin. This is grace, that God judged His Son by putting our sin on Him (see Isaiah 53:4-6). When we believe this by faith the Father now looks upon us as if we had never sinned because the sinless Blood that Jesus shed on the Cross, had the power to wash it all away.

Faith is believing in something even though we cannot see it. It requires faith to believe that what Jesus did in purchasing your eternal salvation is true. As you believe it and give thanks to the Lord for dying for you, you receive it by faith. The Cross of course is a symbol of execution, but now, because of Jesus it is also a symbol of love, of God's extreme love for you and for me. That through it, we can now be declared innocent of all charges and set free from the power of sin. This doesn't mean we won't experience problems or still have to deal with the ongoing effects of our human brokenness, but it does mean that until you eventually leave this world to go to live with the Lord in heaven, you will never be alone. Jesus has promised to never leave you nor forsake you. The Holy Spirit will guide you through life if you allow Him to. This is where faith comes in, we trust in Him even though we can't see Him.

In summer, as I look across the valley, all I can see is the heavy foliage of the trees in the foreground. I can't see the Cross at all, but I know it's there. Then as fall takes hold and the leaves are blown away, the Cross becomes clear against the dark backdrop of the mountains. But when winter arrives and the snow begins to fall, the Cross though huge, disappears from sight because it is painted white. It's still there of course but it cannot be seen. This to me is a great illustration of the Christian life. I know the Cross and its mighty work is there, regardless of the season or whether or not I can see it. And so it is with life's circumstances, whatever you are going through, regardless of your lifestyle or state of mind, the Cross and the saving grace it represents is still there, right where you are, fully available right now for you. As you come to the Lord in the midst of your sin and brokenness, just ask Him to forgive you and He will.

Jesus said to His disciples:

> "I am the way, the truth, and the life. No one comes to the Father except through me. If you had known Me, you would have known my Father also; and from now on you know Him and have seen Him" John 14:6-7.

Jesus was sent on assignment. He came to bring us salvation as the very manifestation of God's love. He also came to show us the Father, introducing us to God's grace and mercy. But He also opened up to us the truth of God's desire to fellowship with mankind by showing us how to walk in obedience to the Father.

Believing in God, having a church membership and a lifetime of being a nice, loving person doesn't add up to walking in obedience to God. The world has drifted further and further away from living in a way that is pleasing to God. So in order to drown out the voice of wisdom that we call conscience, that inner voice that God placed within us, the prevailing voice of our progressive world has learned to shout even louder that, all the world needs to solve its problems is love.

Love is good but on its own leads to the breakdown of all our other good values. Truth is good, but on its own leads to rigid legalism. But if we could view the needs of the world today through the merciful and gracious lens of the Lord Jesus Christ, who is love and truth, then wisdom would bring peace and joy and obedience. This won't happen of course until the Lord returns and sets up His Kingdom.

As Pauline and I look back over our lives together and consider the circuitous route we have taken, it is very humbling to see how God has used us in ever increasing roles in the assignments we were given. Every one of them involved building God's Kingdom in some way.

When a person becomes a child of God, he or she becomes a builder. While we wait for the Lord to return, we keep busy doing the work of the Master so that, at His appearing He can set up His Kingdom. In the Gospel of Luke chapter 21 verses 25 to 36, Jesus gives us a brief insight into some of the things that will be happening in the world shortly before His return. In verses 34, 35 and 36, Jesus takes the time to carefully warn His listeners to watch and pray so that 'Day' will not come unexpected. He talks about the budding of the fig tree being a sign of the soon arrival of summer. Many Bible scholars believe this to point to the coming together of Israel once again as a nation. We know this has happened already. Then Jesus says that when we see these things happening, we should be aware that the Kingdom of God is near.

Jesus talks prophetically about certain signs in the sun, moon and stars and on the earth there will be distress of nations, with perplexity, the sea and the waves roaring, men's hearts failing them from fear and the expectation of those things which are coming on the earth. Then He says, that the powers of the heavens will be shaken. Then they will see the Son of Man coming in a cloud with power and great glory. So for those nay-sayers who think that this is all due to global warming or those who say that this is just more religious fear mongering because it's been said for so many years, Jesus goes on to say "......Now when these things begin to happen, look up and lift up your heads, because your redemption draws near".

We will all stand before the Lord one day, one way or another and none will have an excuse. Jesus Himself gave us fair warning. I choose to believe what God the Son said, exercising my faith in doing so. God cannot lie. He keeps His word and He keeps His promises.

In the meantime, the building goes on. God will continue assigning jobs to His people. Those who understand that 'God's work' is God's work, and that they are simply given the privilege of being involved in what God is doing, they are joyfully resting and abiding in obedience, for it truly is the Lord who is doing His work.

Along with assignments comes responsibility. The outcome of any given assignment should be profitable for God's Kingdom and should bring glory to Him whose work it is. What I learned through those simple words God spoke into my mind that day amongst the trees, "Just keep on knocking, the stuff's in there", was that, when God gives an assignment to a person, He already has all that His servant needs in order to complete the work he has been given. All the servant has to do is to be obedient. God's storehouse is not depleted. The ingredient that makes or breaks the outcome is faith, for without faith, it is impossible to please God. We still had to learn faith even after receiving an assignment. We had to learn to listen for God's guidance, to be available, willing to obey, to ask believing and to wait God's timing.

It's a process that is hard to walk through, especially in the fast paced, impatience of today. So in His love and grace, God lets us deal with our lack of experience by allowing us to just keep on asking, seeking and knocking. He knows what we need of course as this is His work. But He also knows our attitude and motive. He knows if even a legitimate answer to our prayer will have a detrimental effect on us. It could go to our head and cause us to fall into Satan's trap of pride. Humility is hard to learn in the same way patience is. When our heart is right, that will be when God's timing is perfect.

For all those who are seeking God's will and are willing to learn faith, it's sufficient to know that God is not in a hurry and His storehouse is full.

Life in service for God is exciting and full of surprises. This book should be sufficient proof of that. It was written in answer to a young man's question, "Is God still working miracles today?" My answer to him was, "Yes, God is working His miracles in His people's lives all the time as He works to fulfil His will and purpose in what He is doing in His world".

Pauline and I are now settled in our retirement here in British Columbia but we know that there will always be local assignments for us to do for the Lord even in our senior years.

One thing that all of us can and must do no matter our age is pray. Prayer is the greatest force on earth for it can move the hand of God when coupled with faith. We have lived in many different places as we journeyed along the path that God called us to. But there still remains one more majestic destination that burns brightly in our hearts. A destination no-one should miss. It's where all those who have accepted God's offer of His free gift of eternal life will dwell. Our loved ones who believed are there, waiting to greet us. Jesus is there, arms opened wide, waiting to receive us. It's a place where we will live in God's presence forever. It's called heaven.

If we don't see you here on earth, make sure we get to meet up there.

Blessings,

Alan & Pauline.

CPSIA information can be obtained
at www.ICGtesting.com
Printed in the USA
LVOW11s2115050617

537028LV00002B/2/P